Overcoming Eating Disorders

*A Cognitive-Behavioral Treatment
for Bulimia Nervosa
and Binge-Eating Disorder*

Therapist Guide

W. Stewart Agras
Robin F. Apple

OXFORD
UNIVERSITY PRESS

OXFORD
UNIVERSITY PRESS

Oxford University Press, Inc., publishes works that further
Oxford University's objective of excellence
in research, scholarship, and education.

Oxford   New York
Auckland   Cape Town   Dar es Salaam   Hong Kong   Karachi
Kuala Lumpur   Madrid   Melbourne   Mexico City   Nairobi
New Delhi   Shanghai   Taipei   Toronto

With offices in
Argentina   Austria   Brazil   Chile   Czech Republic   France   Greece
Guatemala   Hungary   Italy   Japan   Poland   Portugal   Singapore
South Korea   Switzerland   Thailand   Turkey   Ukraine   Vietnam

Published by Oxford University Press, Inc.
198 Madison Avenue, New York, New York 10016

www.oup.com

Oxford is a registered trademark of Oxford University Press

ISBN-13 978-0-19-518676-5
ISBN 0-19-518676-1

9 8 7 6 5 4 3 2

Printed in the United States of America
on acid-free paper

Contents

▓ Section 1: Introduction to the Therapist Guide and Background Information Concerning Cognitive-Behavioral Therapy

Chapter 1: Introduction 3

The Therapist Guide 3

The Development of the Client Workbook 3

Use of the Therapist Guide and Client Workbook 4

Overview of the Program 4

Why Use a Treatment Manual? 5

Chapter 2: The Nature of Bulimia Nervosa and Binge-Eating Disorder 7

The Syndromes 7

The Etiology of Bulimia 10

The Cognitive-Behavioral Model 11

Chapter 3: The Development of Cognitive-Behavioral Therapy for Bulimia Nervosa 13

Background for the Development of Cognitive-Behavioral Therapy 13

Evidence for the Effectiveness of Cognitive-Behavioral Therapy 14

Comparison With Response Prevention 15

Comparison With Interpersonal Psychotherapy 15

Comparison With Antidepressant Medication 16

Chapter 4: Cognitive-Behavioral Therapy: Some Practical Considerations 17

Which Clients Are Suitable for Cognitive-Behavioral Therapy? 17

Structure of the Therapy Program 18

Structure of the Therapy Sessions 19

Chapter 5: Some Special Issues in Treatment 21

Types of Purging Other Than Vomiting 21

    Laxatives 21

    Diuretics 22

    Ipecac 22

Medical Complications of Bulimia Nervosa 22

Medical Complications of Binge-Eating Disorder 23

Issues Regarding Weight in Bulimia Nervosa 24

    The Underweight Client 24

    The Overweight Client 24

Issues Regarding Weight in Binge-Eating Disorder 25

Chapter 6: Preliminary Evaluation 27

Assessment of the Eating Disorder 27

Assessment of Comorbid Psychopathology 29

Introduction of Treatment Options 29

■ Section 2: The First Phase of Cognitive-Behavioral Therapy

Chapter 7: The First Session 33

The Agenda for the First Session 33

History Taking 34

The Rationale for Cognitive-Behavioral Therapy 35

The Duration and Three-Phase Structure of Therapy 35

The Structure of the Session 36

The Likely Outcome of Treatment 36

Self-Monitoring 37

    The Daily Food Record 37

The Client Workbook 38

Conclusion and Homework 38

Chapter 8: The Second Session 39

The Agenda for the Second Session 39

Review of Daily Food Records 39

Tracking Binge and Purge Behaviors 40

Weekly Weighing and Education About Weight 42

Self-Disclosure 44

The Client With Binge-Eating Disorder 44

Homework 44

Chapter 9: The Third Session 49

The Agenda for the Third Session 49

Review of Self-Monitoring 50

Education Regarding Dietary Restriction, Hunger, and Satiety 50

Education Regarding Self-Induced Vomiting 52

Prescription Regarding Laxative Abuse 53

Prescription Regarding Regular Eating 53

The Client With Binge-Eating Disorder 54

Homework 55

Chapter 10: The Fourth Session 57

The Agenda for the Fourth Session 57

Review of Self-Monitoring 57

Dealing With Adherence Problems 58

Poor Attendance 58

Resistance to Record Keeping 63

Failure to Comply With Behavior Change Prescriptions 64

The Client Who Challenges the Model or Prescriptions 64

The Client With Binge-Eating Disorder 65

Homework 65

Chapter 11: The Remainder of Phase 1 (Sessions 5–9) 69

Meal Planning 71

Eating Style 73

Pleasurable Alternative Activities to Binge Eating and Purging 73

The Duration and Outcome of Phase 1 74

Frequently Encountered Therapist Problems 74

Chapter 12: Assessing Progress 77

Some Reasons for Lack of Progress 78

What to Do About Lack of Progress 79

Add Antidepressant Medication 79

Change to Interpersonal Psychotherapy 79

Poor Compliance 80

When Progress Is Satisfactory 80

Section 3: The Second Phase of Cognitive-Behavioral Therapy

Chapter 13: Introduction to Phase 2 83

Chapter 14: Feared Foods 85
   Feared, Avoided, and Problem Foods 85
   Method for Dealing With Feared Foods 86
   The Client With Binge-Eating Disorder 86
   Homework 88

Chapter 15: Problem Solving 89
   Identifying the Problem 89
   Listing Alternative Solutions to the Problem 89
   Evaluating Each Potential Solution for Its Practicality
      and Likely Effectiveness 90
   Choosing One or More Solutions to the Problem
      Based on the Evaluation 91
   Following Through on the Solution 91
   Reevaluating the Problem and Solutions 91
   Homework 92

Chapter 16: Cognitive Restructuring 93
   Types of Distorted Thinking 94
   Correcting Cognitive Distortions 95
   Homework 98

Chapter 17: Weight and Shape Concerns 99
   Overvaluation of a Slim Figure 103
   Amplification of Ingrained Beliefs About Being Fat 103
   Homework 105

Chapter 18: Interpersonal Triggers and Transient Negative Mood . . 107

Section 4: The Third Phase of Cognitive-Behavioral Therapy: Maintenance of Change

Chapter 19: Relapse Prevention 113
   The Successful Client 114
   The Unsuccessful Client 115

Homework During Phase 3 116

References 117

Figures

Figure 2.1. Cognitive-Behavioral Model of Bulimia Nervosa
and Binge-Eating Disorder 12

Figure 8.1. Example of a Daily Food Record for a Client With
Bulimia Nervosa 41

Figure 8.2. Weight Change Record for Use
With Binge-Eating Disorder 43

Figure 8.3. Weight Change in Clients With Binge-Eating Disorder 45

Figure 8.4. Example of a Daily Food Record for a Client With
Binge-Eating Disorder 46

Figure 9.1. Example of a Full Day's Daily Food Record for a Client
With Bulimia Nervosa 51

Figure 10.1. Example of a Daily Food Record for a Client With
Bulimia Nervosa Showing Grazing and a Long Interval
Between Eating Episodes 59

Figure 10.2. Example of a Daily Food Record for a Client With
Bulimia Nervosa Showing Progress Toward Regular Eating 61

Figure 10.3. Example of a Daily Food Record for a Client With
Binge-Eating Disorder Showing Eating Patterns Similar to
Bulimia Nervosa 66

Figure 11.1. Example of a Daily Food Record for a Client
With Bulimia Nervosa Showing Progress in Restrictive
Eating Patterns 70

Figure 11.2. Example of a Daily Food Record for a Client
With Bulimia Nervosa Showing Regular Eating Patterns 72

Figure 11.3. The Time Course of Improvement for Six Clients
With Bulimia Nervosa Who Recovered With
Cognitive-Behavioral Therapy 75

Figure 14.1. Example Feared and Problem Foods List 87

Series Introduction

The psychosocial treatment program in this Therapist Guide is part of a series of empirically supported treatment programs. The purpose of the series is to disseminate knowledge about specific interventions for which systematic research studies indicate effectiveness. This treatment program, along with others in the series, has been clearly demonstrated to have empirical support for its efficacy in treating the particular condition you are addressing. However, clinicians operate with a wide variety of clients with different characteristics who are treated in different types of settings. Thus, the manner in which the treatment program is implemented will be the decision of the treating clinician with his or her unparalleled knowledge of the local clinical situation and the particular client under care. Although some data indicate that allegiance to the treatment protocol produces the best results in a variety of clinical settings, only the treating clinician is in a position to judge the degree of flexibility required to achieve optimal results.

We sincerely hope that you find the psychosocial treatment program, of which this Therapist Guide forms an integral part, useful in your clinical practice. This Therapist Guide is meant to accompany various clinical materials that you would be prescribing for clients in the implementation of this program. This Therapist Guide is designed to assist clinicians in the systematic and sequential administration of the particular treatment program being implemented. As such it will highlight relevant information and exercises to which the clinician will want to attend in sessions. The guide also presents typical problems that may arise in the implementation of specific therapeutic procedures and suggests means for solving these problems. Thus, therapists may want to review the brief individual chapters corresponding to each therapeutic session or intervention prior to conducting sessions, perhaps while reviewing case notes.

Although the Therapist Guide is not a full description of the theoretical approach and empirical work that supports this treatment, references for additional information are provided. We encourage review of these readings for a comprehensive understanding. Please let us know if you have suggestions for improving our systems for helping you deliver effective psychosocial treatments for clients under your care.

David H. Barlow
Boston, Massachusetts

About the Authors

W. Stewart Agras received his medical degree from University College, London University, UK, and has published over 300 articles and chapters. He is currently Professor of Psychiatry at the Stanford University School of Medicine, and Director of the Psychiatry Outpatient Clinics. In addition, he is Director of the Behavioral Medicine Program at Stanford. He is a Past President of the Association for the Advancement of Behavior Therapy (AABT) and of the Society for Behavioral Medicine, and he has been a Fellow at the Center for Advanced Study in the Behavioral Sciences on two occasions. His research during the past 15 years has primarily focused on eating disorders, including epidemiologic, laboratory, and clinical outcome studies, with the aim of advancing knowledge and treatment of the eating disorders.

Robin F. Apple completed her PhD at the University of California, Los Angeles and her postdoctoral fellowship at the Oregon Health Sciences University. Since 1993, she has been on staff in the Behavioral Medicine Clinic, Department of Psychiatry, Stanford University Medical Center. Dr. Apple has participated in a multicenter study investigating the effectiveness of interpersonal and cognitive-behavioral therapies for the treatment of Bulimia Nervosa. She has also taken part in numerous other clinical experiences, as well as teaching and writing projects, which focus on the treatment of bulimia and binge-eating disorder and the match between client and therapy model.

Acknowledgments

The authors gratefully acknowledge the contributions of the many staff members of the Behavioral Medicine Clinic at Stanford University who over the past 15 years have contributed to the various revisions of cognitive-behavioral therapy manuals produced for research purposes. We have also learned much from our patients—both those treated in the clinic, and those who have generously given of their time in the several controlled trials of cognitive-behavioral therapy for Bulimia Nervosa and binge-eating disorder that have been carried out over the years at Stanford.

We also acknowledge the help of colleagues at other centers, particularly Christopher Fairburn, MD, at Oxford University, Katherine Halmi, MD, at Cornell University, James Mitchell, MD, at the University of Minnesota, and Terence Wilson, PhD, at Rutgers University, with whom we have been involved in collaborative multicenter trials of the effectiveness of cognitive-behavioral therapy. During these trials therapists have been supervised closely, allowing various therapeutic procedures to be better detailed. We are grateful to Dr. Fairburn for providing an earlier manual detailing cognitive-behavioral therapy for bulimia, on which this manual is based. The National Institutes of Health, and more recently the McKnight Foundation, have provided support for our research.

Finally, we wish to acknowledge the efforts and contributions made by various individuals at The Psychological Corporation, especially John Dilworth, President; Joanne Lenke, PhD, Executive Vice President; and Aurelio Prifitera, PhD, Vice President and Director of the Psychological Measurement Group. As Project Director, Sandra Prince-Embury, PhD, has contributed to the high quality of the Therapist Guide. Special appreciation is also extended to those persons whose diligent and meticulous efforts were essential in preparing the Therapist Guide. Among these individuals are Stephanie Tong, MA, Research Assistant; Kathy Overstreet, Senior Editor; Vicki Veselka, Editor; and Javier Flores, Designer.

Introduction to the Therapist Guide and Background Information Concerning Cognitive-Behavioral Therapy

Introduction

The Therapist Guide

This Therapist Guide contains background information essential to the understanding of Bulimia Nervosa, binge-eating disorder, and their treatment with cognitive-behavioral therapy. It presents a treatment program, including the details of specific therapy sessions and phases of therapy, that is based on research that has demonstrated effectiveness. Frequent review of this Therapist Guide is recommended in order to maximize consistency and effectiveness. The accompanying Client Workbook entitled *Overcoming Eating Disorders: A Cognitive-Behavioral Treatment for Bulimia Nervosa and Binge-Eating Disorder* should also be read by the therapist, because it contains information linked to specific treatment sessions and procedures. This program is not recommended for treating clients with current diagnoses of Anorexia Nervosa.

The Development of the Client Workbook

The Therapist Guide and Client Workbook derive from several years of controlled clinical trials of the treatment of Bulimia Nervosa and binge-eating disorder at Stanford University. Manuals were produced for each of these trials with each revision based on the experience of conducting therapy in controlled trials and of treating clients in the Eating Disorders Clinic. Further development derives from collaborative work with colleagues such as Christopher Fairburn, MD, at Oxford University, Katherine Halmi, MD, at Cornell University, James Mitchell, MD, at the University of Minnesota, and Terence Wilson, PhD, at Rutgers University, among others. In addition, the clinical and research literature on Bulimia Nervosa and binge-eating disorder has led to further refinements of the treatment approach.

Use of the Therapist Guide and Client Workbook

The Therapist Guide is intended for use by qualified therapists who have had some experience in the assessment and treatment of eating disorders. It may also be used by the therapist in training under the guidance of experienced trainers. The Client Workbook is intended for the use of the client with Bulimia Nervosa or binge-eating disorder under the supervision of a qualified professional. It is not intended for use as a self-help manual. It should be noted that in the Therapist Guide, there are examples of completed Daily Food Records to use as a guide for client self-monitoring.

The treatment program described may be conducted either in the context of individual or group therapy with the necessary adjustments dictated by the form of therapy. To date, because treatment of overweight is usually provided in a group format, all the published controlled research with clients who have binge-eating disorder has been carried out in that format. However, this is not a necessary format, and experience in the authors' clinic suggests that individual therapy is both effective and more comfortable for many clients with binge-eating disorder.

Overview of the Program

In general, the research findings regarding the treatment of Bulimia Nervosa and binge-eating disorder suggest that although several types of therapy may be useful in the treatment of these disorders, cognitive-behavioral therapy can be considered the treatment of choice at the present time. Cognitive-behavioral therapy has been found to be more effective than other forms of therapy such as non-directive therapy, focal psychotherapy, psychodynamic treatment, stress management, and antidepressant medication.

The treatment program is intended to be carried out in 18–20 sessions spread over a 6-month interval. Individual sessions are usually 50 minutes in length, and group sessions are usually 90 minutes long. In adapting the treatment to a group format it may be useful to assess progress by holding individual sessions with the client before treatment begins (analogous to the Session 1 format described in Chapter 7), at a point midway through therapy (see Chapter 12), and at the end of treatment. Although various timing patterns can be used, the most practical seems to be to hold more frequent sessions in the beginning of treatment (for example, four sessions in the first 2 weeks), followed by weekly sessions, with the last few sessions being held at 2-week intervals. Holding more frequent sessions in the first 2 weeks allows the therapist and client to come to grips with the problem more quickly, and provides an opportunity for many clients to experience rapidly the benefits of changing their behavior. The advantage of the longer interval toward the end of treatment is that clients have more time to experience and practice overcoming residual problems.

Not all clients need the full 18–20 sessions of treatment. It is often the case that clients become binge-and purge-free during the first few sessions of therapy, allowing the therapist and client to move into the later phases of treatment more quickly, hence reducing the total therapeutic time. All clients should, however, be exposed to all the elements contained in each of the three phases of treatment described in Chapter 4 of this Therapist Guide. This allows for a full evaluation of the client's problem areas and for adequate treatment of each of the problems, as well as preparing the client for maintenance of his or her improvements. Conversely, if a client demonstrates little or no improvement in the first 10 sessions, then the therapist should consider alternative approaches to treatment as described in Chapter 12.

Why Use a Treatment Manual?

There are benefits to both the therapist and client from using a manual-based therapy. First, the structure, although flexible, ensures that the treatment procedures are sequenced in an optimal fashion and that all the components of therapy are adequately covered. Second, a manual keeps both the therapist and client on track. Without the benefit of a manual it is easy for a considerable amount of therapy time to be devoted to issues that are not central to the treatment of Bulimia Nervosa or binge-eating disorder. Third, the procedures described in this Therapist

Guide have been tested in controlled outcome studies, hence both the client and therapist can have some confidence that the treatment works (Agras, Schneider, Arnow, Raeburn, & Telch, 1989; Agras, et al., 1992; Agras, Rossiter, et al., 1994; Agras, Telch, et al., 1994; Agras, Telch, Arnow, Eldredge, & Marnell, in press; Telch, Agras, Rossiter, Wilfley, & Kenardy, 1990; Wilfley, et al., 1993).

There are additional benefits for the client. The client can read the Client Workbook ahead of each session, to better prepare for what is to come. The Client Workbook can also be read following each session to reinforce points covered in the recent session or in past sessions. Moreover, during the later phases of therapy or after completing therapy, clients can refer to it for guidance on maintaining their gains. Some clients appreciate the fact that their families can read portions of it, thus gaining insight into the eating disorder and its treatment.

CHAPTER 2

The Nature of Bulimia Nervosa and Binge-Eating Disorder

The Syndromes

Binge eating, common to both Bulimia Nervosa and binge-eating disorder, is characterized by a sense of loss of control over eating. This sense of losing control appears to consist of negative and sometimes conflicting thoughts and feelings about food. The cognitive components may consist of thoughts such as "I don't want to do this; I shouldn't be eating like this," or "I'm being a pig again," as well as positive thoughts such as "I really deserve a treat, so I should eat the ice cream." The affective components may consist of an overwhelming urge to eat accompanied by positive feelings sometimes described as a thrill or as excitement, and negative feelings such as anxiety, anger, guilt, or depression. The negative transient moods of anxiety, anger, or depression often result from unsatisfactory interpersonal interactions, with the negative mood triggering a binge episode. The most commonly reported trigger for a binge is a transient negative mood, followed in frequency by dietary restriction and feelings of hunger and/or deprivation.

Binges may be large or small, in the client with Bulimia Nervosa averaging about 1500 kcal, and in the client with binge-eating disorder about 1000 kcal. Binge size ranges in both disorders from 100 to 7000 or more kcal. Large, or objective, binges are differentiated from small, or subjective, binges. For example, the *Diagnostic and Statistical Manual of Mental Disorders, Fourth Edition* (*DSM–IV*; American Psychiatric Association, 1994) requires that binges consist of eating a large amount of food.

The prognostic significance of the size of the binge is unknown at present. However, it is clear that subjective binges are experienced by the client as being as upsetting as objective binges. Some evidence (Smith, Marcus, & Kaye, 1992) suggests that objective binges are the first to disappear during treatment, followed by subjective binges.

The foods eaten in binges vary widely, but typically consist of sweet (often high fat) easily swallowed foods, such as ice cream, cookies, breads, cereals, and so on. Some clients, however, binge on several servings of a main course. Clients with Bulimia Nervosa often drink large quantities of fluids to facilitate self-induced vomiting.

The average age for the onset of binge eating in both Bulimia Nervosa and binge-eating disorder is 19 years, usually followed a few months later by purging in Bulimia Nervosa, and by gradual weight gain in binge-eating disorder (Fairburn, Cooper, & Cooper, 1986). However, about 10% of clients with Bulimia Nervosa are overweight, whereas some 25–30% of clients have a past history of Anorexia Nervosa (Agras, et al., 1989; Agras, et al., 1992). Excessive exercise, aimed at control of weight and shape, is also common in Bulimia Nervosa.

In Bulimia Nervosa, purging follows binge eating. Purging is usually accomplished by self-induced vomiting or the use of laxatives, or both, and less commonly by diuretic abuse. Occasionally, clients with bulimia will chew binge food and then spit it out. Between 20% and 30% of clients with binge-eating disorder have purged in the past, often meeting criteria for Bulimia Nervosa at that time (Yanovski, 1993). Others have tried to purge but find that they cannot do it, or find it repulsive.

The *DSM–IV* (1994) diagnostic criteria for Bulimia Nervosa, which are shown on the next page, include binge eating and purging, on average, at least twice weekly for a period of 3 months. Binge eating is defined as (a) eating, in a discrete period of time, an amount of food which is definitely larger than most people would eat during a similar period of time under similar circumstances, and (b) a sense of lack of control over eating during the episode, e.g., a feeling that one cannot stop eating or control what or how much one is eating.

DSM–IV (1994) Diagnostic Criteria for Bulimia Nervosa

A. Recurrent episodes of binge eating. An episode of binge eating is characterized by both of the following:

   (1) eating, in a discrete period of time (e.g., within any 2-hour period), an amount of food that is definitely larger than most people would eat during a similar period of time and under similar circumstances

   (2) a sense of lack of control over eating during the episode (e.g., a feeling that one cannot stop eating or control what or how much one is eating)

B. Recurrent inappropriate compensatory behavior in order to prevent weight gain, such as self-induced vomiting; misuse of laxatives, diuretics, enemas, or other medications; fasting; or excessive exercise.

C. The binge eating and inappropriate compensatory behaviors both occur, on average, at least twice a week for 3 months.

D. Self-evaluation is unduly influenced by body shape and weight.

E. The disturbance does not occur exclusively during episodes of Anorexia Nervosa.

Specify type:

   Purging Type: during the current episode of Bulimia Nervosa, the person has regularly engaged in self-induced vomiting or the misuse of laxatives, diuretics, or enemas

   Nonpurging Type: during the current episode of Bulimia Nervosa, the person has used other inappropriate compensatory behaviors, such as fasting or excessive exercise, but has not regularly engaged in self-induced vomiting or the misuse of laxatives, diuretics, or enemas

The diagnostic criteria for binge-eating disorder in *DSM–IV* (1994) are denoted as research criteria for further study. The criteria for a binge are identical with those for Bulimia Nervosa. However, the syndrome includes behaviors associated with binge eating (of which at least three should be present), including eating more rapidly than usual; eating until uncomfortably full; eating large amounts of food when not hungry; eating alone; and feeling disgusted, depressed, or guilty after binge eating. In addition, marked emotional distress concerning the binge eating should be present. Binge eating should occur at an average frequency of at least 2 days per week for a period of 6 months. Days, rather than episodes, are used in binge-eating disorder because when a binge is not ended by purging, there is a tendency for such episodes to be less well demarcated. Such binges are therefore not always remembered as distinct episodes. Some clients with binge-eating disorder tend to eat small amounts of food over several hours, a pattern known as *grazing*.

Clients who do not meet the full criteria for Bulimia Nervosa or binge-eating disorder because they binge eat less frequently than twice a week, or do not experience large binges, are classified as having Eating Disorder Not Otherwise Specified.

Both Bulimia Nervosa and binge-eating disorder are frequently accompanied by comorbid psychopathology that may need to be treated separately from the eating disorder. The syndromes most frequently associated with eating disorders are: Major Depressive Disorder; anxiety disorders, including Panic Disorder and Social Phobia; personality disorders, especially the Cluster B disorders (*DSM–IV;* 1994) associated with emotional instability and impulsive behaviors; and alcohol or drug abuse or both.

The Etiology of Bulimia

Studies of Bulimia Nervosa find that the disorder tends to run in families, suggesting either genetic transmission or psychological factors affecting family members (Kendler, et al., 1991). Twin studies suggest that Bulimia Nervosa is heritable, accounting for perhaps half the variance in etiology, although the nature of what is inherited is unknown (Kendler, et al., 1991). Some studies suggest that brain serotonin levels may be lower than normal in the client with Bulimia Nervosa, and that the high carbohydrate intake tends to alleviate that situation (Christensen, 1993;

Lieberman, Wurtman, & Chew, 1986). Low serotonin levels may also be associated with depression, a frequent accompaniment of bulimia.

Environmental factors also appear important in the etiology of bulimia. The pressure on women to achieve a thin body appears to have increased in the last 25 years. Coincidentally, there has been a sudden rise in the number of cases of Bulimia Nervosa presenting to clinics across the Western world in the early 1970s (Garner, Garfinkel, Schwartz, & Thompson, 1980). This appears to be due to a portrayal of ever-thinner ideal body types in the media combined with a rapid increase in the number of articles describing various types of diets. Other factors predisposing to Bulimia Nervosa may be a family history of obesity, teasing about weight and shape by peers during adolescence, and low self-esteem from any cause (Pike, 1995; Striegel-Moore, 1993). However, it appears that psychological influences within the family are specific to particular individuals and are not shared by all children within the family.

The Cognitive-Behavioral Model

The cognitive-behavioral model of Bulimia Nervosa and binge-eating disorder is outlined in Figure 2.1. One of the key features of the disorder is dietary restriction, which in turn leads to hunger, eventually to disinhibition of eating, and finally to binge eating. Dieting in both the client with Bulimia Nervosa and the client with binge-eating disorder often follows a period of actual or perceived weight gain. It seems likely that young women with low self-esteem deriving from a variety of causes are more likely to become overly concerned about their weight and shape, perhaps restricting food intake to a greater extent than their peers.

Cognitive influences are found in perceptions of weight and shape and rules about what weight and shape should be, rules about what foods to eat or to avoid, and rules about amounts of food to eat. Often there are also faulty perceptions of having eaten too much when the amount is within the normal range. Negative mood, often stemming from faulty interpersonal interactions, also leads to binge eating. Indeed, studies suggest that 70% of binge episodes are triggered by a transient negative mood (Arnow, Kenardy, & Agras, 1992; Bruce & Agras, 1992). Binge eating is followed by purging in individuals who have bulimia, and by guilt in both Bulimia Nervosa and binge-eating disorder, with a consequent lowering of self-esteem.

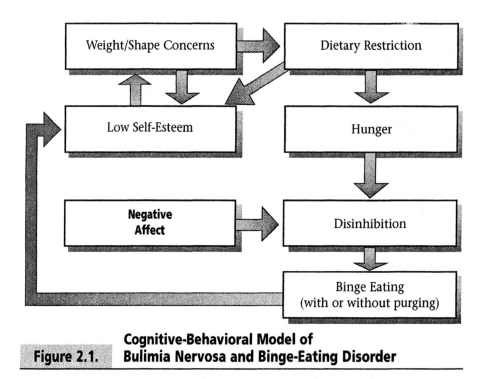

Figure 2.1. **Cognitive-Behavioral Model of Bulimia Nervosa and Binge-Eating Disorder**

CHAPTER 3

The Development of Cognitive-Behavioral Therapy for Bulimia Nervosa

Background for the Development of Cognitive-Behavioral Therapy

Cognitive-behavioral therapy (CBT) as applied to Bulimia Nervosa was developed and refined at several research centers both in the US and abroad. The model of Bulimia Nervosa outlined in the previous chapter was developed from clinical observation and from descriptive studies of factors leading to binge eating and purging. The treatment program was initially derived from cognitive-behavioral therapies applied to disorders such as depression, and from behavior therapies for weight loss.

As the treatment was tested and refined in both the clinic and in controlled studies, three main elements of treatment were formulated. First, treatment targets behavior changes to regulate the chronic dieting in which clients with Bulimia Nervosa engage, which is hypothesized to lead to binge eating. This first phase of therapy focuses on helping clients with bulimia learn to eat at regular times, consuming three meals and two snacks each day. This strategy reduces the dietary restriction that tends to trigger binge eating. It appears to be the critical element of treatment, i.e., necessary but not sufficient for recovery. The second phase addresses additional triggers for binge eating as well as factors maintaining binge eating, such as overvalued ideas about weight and shape. In this phase of treatment new procedures such as problem solving and cognitive restructuring are introduced. The final phase of treatment clarifies the changes already made and develops a plan to cope with residual problems.

Evidence for the Effectiveness of Cognitive-Behavioral Therapy

Nearly 30 controlled studies of cognitive-behavioral therapy attest to its effectiveness in both Bulimia Nervosa and more recently in binge-eating disorder. Cognitive-behavioral therapy has proven more effective than no treatment, non-directive psychotherapy, manual-based psycho-dynamic therapy, stress management, and antidepressant medication (Agras, et al., 1992; Fairburn, Kirk, O'Connor, & Cooper, 1986; Garner, et al., 1993; Laessle, et al., 1991; Mitchell, et al., 1990). Research demonstrates that about half the clients receiving CBT stop binge eating and purging by the completion of this treatment, and attitudes regarding weight and shape also improve. An additional percentage continue to improve following treatment, leading to a total "cure" rate of about 65% (Agras, Rossiter, et al., 1994). Follow-up studies demonstrate maintenance of improvement up to 5 years post treatment, although some clients may have a brief return of symptoms from time to time (Agras, Rossiter, et al., 1994; Agras, et al., in press; Fairburn, Jones, Peveler, Hope, & O'Connor, 1993). Although far fewer studies of cognitive-behavioral therapy have been reported for binge-eating disorder, similar results can be expected.

Because overweight or demonstrable obesity usually accompanies binge-eating disorder, weight loss treatment may be useful following successful completion of CBT. It has been shown that clients who stop binge eating are able to lose a modest amount of weight and to maintain that weight loss for a year post treatment (Agras, et al., in press). In contrast, clients who do not stop binge eating gain weight during both the treatment and follow-up periods (Agras, et al., in press). For some time it was felt that weight loss programs might be harmful for clients with binge-eating disorder, because dietary restraint often leads to binge eating. It appears, however, that clients with binge-eating disorder are not highly restrained. For example, there is no difference between overweight binge eating clients and weight-matched non–binge eaters on measures of dietary restraint, although the two groups differ on other variables, e.g., weight and shape concerns and comorbid psychopathology (Eldredge & Agras, 1996; Garner, Garfinkel, Schwartz, & Thompson, 1980). It seems likely that CBT combined with a modest weight loss program allows the overweight client with binge-eating disorder to achieve modest but useful weight losses.

Comparison With Response Prevention

Leitenberg and his colleagues (Leitenberg, Rosen, Gross, Nudelman, & Vara, 1988) at the University of Vermont applied exposure to binge foods followed by response prevention, a procedure successfully used in treating compulsive rituals, to Bulimia Nervosa. In this procedure the client consumes enough binge food during a therapy session to bring on the desire to purge. The client then stays in the therapy session until the urge dissipates, thus learning that they can control the desire to purge. It is assumed that binge eating will be reduced once the desire to purge has been eliminated.

Initial studies (Leitenberg, et al., 1988) demonstrated some success with this procedure. However, a later study (Agras, et al., 1989) demonstrated that adding response prevention to CBT led to poorer results when compared to CBT alone. The worse results, as a later study demonstrated (Wilson, Eldredge, Smith, & Niles, 1991), were due to the fact that less CBT was used in the combined condition. Nonetheless, gradual exposure to feared foods (most clients with Bulimia Nervosa have a long list of such foods), but not response prevention, has been adopted as a standard component of CBT. This seems reasonable because avoidance of feared foods is an aspect of chronic dieting.

Comparison With Interpersonal Psychotherapy

Fairburn (Fairburn, et al., 1991) at Oxford University found that interpersonal psychotherapy (IPT), specifically adapted for the treatment of Bulimia Nervosa, was as effective as cognitive-behavioral therapy. This result was replicated in binge-eating disorder in a study conducted at Stanford University (Wilfley, et al., 1993). Interpersonal psychotherapy, which was first introduced as a nonintrospective, short-term psychological treatment for depression (Klerman, Weissman, Rounsaville, & Chevron, 1984), focuses exclusively on correcting current faulty interpersonal relationships. Moreover, in its adaptation to Bulimia Nervosa, the eating disorder is only discussed in the first four "diagnostic" sessions in which the relationships between interpersonal events and the eating disorder are explored. In the remaining sessions, the eating disorder is essentially ignored, and the focus of treatment is exclusively in the interpersonal domain. The apparently favorable results of treatment with IPT remind us that negative affect, often stemming from faulty interpersonal interactions, is an important trigger for binge eating. Such interpersonal interactions and the accompanying negative affect form a focus of exploration in the second phase of CBT.

Comparison With Antidepressant Medication

Contemporary with the development of CBT, Pope at Harvard University (Pope, Hudson, Jonas, & Yurgelun-Todd, 1983) found that the antidepressant imipramine was more effective than placebo in reducing binge eating in Bulimia Nervosa. Since that time both the tricyclic antidepressants (e.g., imipramine, desipramine) and the serotonin reuptake inhibitors (e.g., fluoxetine) have been shown to be more effective than placebo. More recently, the antidepressants have been demonstrated to be effective in binge-eating disorder.

However, two studies (Agras, et al., 1992; Mitchell, et al., 1990) have now found that antidepressants when combined with CBT do not improve the outcome of treatment in reducing binge eating in Bulimia Nervosa. In one study (Mitchell, et al., 1990), depression was improved more in those receiving medication, and in the other study (Agras, et al., 1992), dietary preoccupation was reduced more in the combined group than in the group receiving CBT alone. A recent controlled study (Agras, Telch, et al., 1994) found that the use of an antidepressant in binge-eating disorder led to superior weight losses as compared to the use of CBT alone. These findings suggest that the primary approach to the treatment of both Bulimia Nervosa and binge-eating disorder should be cognitive-behavioral therapy, and that medication might be added for clients who do not respond to CBT.

Cognitive-Behavioral Therapy: Some Practical Considerations

Which Clients Are Suitable for Cognitive-Behavioral Therapy?

As Chapter 3 demonstrated, cognitive-behavioral therapy has been shown to be effective both for Bulimia Nervosa and for binge-eating disorder. There is also reason to believe that clients with subclinical variants of these disorders respond to such treatment, for example, clients who binge eat less than twice each week on average, or clients whose binges are small. There have been few factors predictive of poor outcome. In the case of Bulimia Nervosa, the most common predictor of poor outcome has been low weight during adolescence often associated with a past history of clinical or subclinical Anorexia Nervosa. Hence, a history of Anorexia Nervosa, although not a contraindication for treatment, may suggest a poorer outcome for treatment. Additional treatment as discussed in Chapter 12 may be necessary for such clients. However, as previously mentioned, the treatment described in this Therapist Guide is not recommended for treatment of clients currently diagnosed with Anorexia Nervosa.

Some other factors merit assessment in regard to the suitability of a particular client for treatment. When substance abuse or dependence coexist with Bulimia Nervosa or binge-eating disorder, it is usually best to treat the alcohol or drug problem before treating the bulimia. A concurrent diagnosis of severe depression also merits treatment before beginning treatment for bulimia, because the depression will interfere with the client's ability to adhere to the treatment recommendations. In this regard it should be remembered that CBT requires clients to take risks by changing habits and assessing the results of such changes. Clients should be in a position to give treatment a high priority for several months. If other major life issues or changes that would interfere with treatment are apparent, they should be discussed in detail with the client, and if necessary treatment should be deferred until these issues are resolved.

Structure of the Therapy Program

The usual course of cognitive-behavioral therapy takes some 18–20 sessions spread over 6 months. The therapy is divided into three distinct but overlapping phases. The length of each phase and the degree of overlap between one phase and another is determined by the client's progress.

It is assumed that before beginning treatment a thorough assessment of the client's problem and of any comorbid psychopathology has been made, and that the client has agreed to treatment.

Phase 1. Although not mandatory, it has been found that completing the first four sessions in a 2-week period is helpful in providing a rapid start to treatment and facilitating the development of a satisfactory working relationship between client and therapist. The first aim of this phase of treatment is to use self-monitoring to clarify the details of the client's eating habits, using these data to present the model of Bulimia Nervosa to the client. The main elements of the model are that dietary restraint (usually quite obvious from the client's history and self-monitoring) leads to excessive hunger and eventually to loss of control over eating and to binge eating. For the client with Bulimia Nervosa this leads to purging (compounding dietary restriction with the caloric loss) and to guilt, with subsequent lowering of self-esteem. For the client with binge-eating disorder, the excess calories consumed while binge eating lead to inexorable weight gain, leading in turn to increased concern about weight and shape, and to guilt about gaining weight. To overcome this pattern of eating, i.e., alternating dietary restriction and binge eating, the client is gradually encouraged to eat at regular intervals (by the clock) three meals and two snacks each day. Formal problem solving may be introduced in this phase to help overcome specific problems, and toward the end of this phase work begins on the consumption of a broader array of foods. By the end of Phase 1, which usually lasts about eight sessions, the client should be eating regularly, reducing dietary restriction, and manifesting less frequent binge eating (and purging).

Phase 2. While the general aims of Phase 1 continue to be implemented in the second phase of treatment, the focus shifts to other triggers of binge eating. Goals of this phase include broadening food choices to decrease the number of feared and avoided foods, formal problem solving as a general tool to accomplish the goals of this phase, formal cognitive restructuring of rigid food rules and distorted perceptions of shape and weight, using behavioral tasks such as observing the shape and weight of other women to reduce concerns about weight and shape, and identifying interpersonal triggers that are often associated with negative mood.

Phase 3. The last three sessions are usually devoted in part to a review of the positive changes that have occurred during treatment as a result of the behavior changes made by the client. In addition, residual problems are defined, and the client is encouraged to form a plan to deal with these problems and to avoid lapses. At least some of these problems will already have been dealt with in the second phase of treatment. To allow more time for such residual problems to surface, it is suggested that the final three sessions be held at 2-week intervals.

Structure of the Therapy Sessions

Therapy proceeds more smoothly when the session is well structured. Hence, each session should be structured as follows. After an initial greeting and a general inquiry as to how things are going, the homework set at the end of the last session should be reviewed. This will require that the client and therapist review the self-monitoring records completed since the last session. Depending on the record review and upon the phase and progress of therapy, the therapist should then set a specific agenda for the session. This should form the main work for the session, and should be followed by a review of the main points covered, which should naturally lead to setting specific homework to be done before the next session.

CHAPTER 5

Some Special Issues in Treatment

Types of Purging Other Than Vomiting

Laxatives

Many clients with Bulimia Nervosa use laxatives in addition to self-induced vomiting as a form of purging. More rarely, laxatives may be the only method of purging used. The most favored laxatives are those that stimulate the bowel, and clients may use large amounts of these medications following a binge.

It should be noted that laxatives are an extremely ineffective method of ridding the body of calories because most of the calories have been absorbed by the time the food reaches the lower bowel. At most, laxatives provide a false illusion of "emptying the body" of excess calories. Unfortunately, the bowel adapts to the use of bowel-stimulating laxatives. Constipation ensues if the laxative is stopped, thus maintaining the laxative habit. Although calories are retained, the chronic use of laxatives can lead to dehydration and potassium depletion.

Experience suggests that the most effective method of dealing with the use of laxatives as a method of purging is to stop their use abruptly. The client should be warned of the effects of stopping, e.g., constipation, bloating, abdominal discomfort, but also reassured that such effects are relatively short-lived, ending in about 10 days in the majority of cases. Prescription of bulk laxatives, or a diet high in fiber, may be helpful in returning the bowel to normal function. Some clients cannot tolerate the effects of sudden cessation of laxative use, and consequently must be withdrawn gradually on a schedule set jointly by the client and the therapist.

Diuretics

Less commonly, clients with Bulimia Nervosa abuse diuretics to decrease feelings of bloating. Those who abuse diuretics also hold the mistaken belief that they can better maintain weight and shape using diuretics. Chronic use leads to renal damage. Renal failure may eventually occur, necessitating dialysis. Hence, clients who have used diuretics in large doses for a considerable period of time should have their level of renal function evaluated.

Experience again suggests that stopping the diuretic abruptly is the best approach to this method of purging. The client should be warned that they may experience water retention with bloating and swelling of some body parts.

Ipecac

Occasionally clients who have difficulty inducing vomiting may use ipecac, which causes nausea and vomiting. Chronic use of ipecac is dangerous and may lead to cardiomyopathy (deterioration of the cardiac muscle) and heart failure. Because of these potential complications clients should be advised to stop the use of ipecac immediately.

Medical Complications of Bulimia Nervosa

Detailed medical investigations of clients with Bulimia Nervosa reveal only a few regularly found problems. Dental and periodontal problems occur most frequently. Because of the sugars consumed, and acid in the mouth after vomiting, severe erosion of dental enamel may occur. In the more severe cases, metal fillings can be seen protruding from the tooth because the enamel around the filling has been eroded. Multiple dental caries are often found. Periodontal infections may also occur, sometimes with erosion of the bone surrounding teeth. If clients with Bulimia Nervosa are not seeing a dentist regularly, they should be advised to do so.

The next most frequent problem is swelling of the salivary glands that looks similar to mumps. Such swelling is transient and requires no treatment.

About 5% of clients with Bulimia Nervosa are found to have a low serum potassium level, hypokalemia, due to purging. Hypokalemia may be associated with marked feelings of weakness, difficulty concentrating, and fainting. Low levels of potassium are associated with changes in the electrocardiogram. In combination with low weight, as in low-weight clients with Bulimia Nervosa, they may lead to fatal cardiac arrhythmia. Hypokalemia can be reversed with a prescription for a simple potassium supplement.

The malnutrition associated with Bulimia Nervosa, including depletion of fat, is often associated with undue sensitivity to cold, dryness and coarsening of the skin, and hair loss. When combined with low weight, a sign of severe dietary restriction, osteoporosis may occur. Osteoporosis occasionally leads to fractures, especially in clients with Bulimia Nervosa who engage in heavy exercise. Dietary restriction may also lead to iron deficiency anemia.

Rare complications include spitting up blood from small tears in the esophagus consequent to purging, and cases of rupture of the stomach have been reported following very large binges. Foreign objects may also be swallowed occasionally in the course of a binge. For example, a client once swallowed a spoon in a particularly voracious eating episode, necessitating surgical removal.

Medical Complications of Binge-Eating Disorder

Clients with binge-eating disorder tend to gain weight steadily. It was demonstrated in a group of clients that as adiposity increased, the percentage of clients diagnosed as having binge-eating disorder increased. In most clinical samples of overweight individuals between one quarter and one third will meet criteria for binge-eating disorder. Hence, the medical complications associated with this disorder are those associated with overweight and obesity. Among the conditions frequently seen in such clients are essential hypertension, diabetes, and hyperlipidemia. Other complications include osteoarthritis, gall bladder disease, and menstrual disturbances. Finally, it should be remembered that in addition to the guilt that these individuals feel about their disorder they will also encounter social stigmatization because of being overweight, both of which will lead to lowering of self-esteem.

Issues Regarding Weight in Bulimia Nervosa

Clients with Bulimia Nervosa vary considerably in their weights. They range from a body mass index (BMI; calculated as weight in kilograms, divided by height in meters squared) similar to that seen in Anorexia Nervosa (17.5 kg/m^2), to a BMI that indicates obesity (greater than 27 kg/m^2). The latter comprises some 10% of the clinical sample of clients with Bulimia Nervosa. Because weight and shape concerns are a cardinal feature of Bulimia Nervosa, clients at different points in this range will have different perceptions of the effects of treatment.

The Underweight Client

Apart from the potential nutritional problems noted above, the under-weight client often demonstrates marked resistance regarding the potential of weight gain once dietary restriction, purging, and excessive exercise are abandoned. Such clients may be excessively fearful of changing their eating habits in the first phase of treatment, and hence may demonstrate less improvement than is usual during the first phase. Although the therapist can provide some reassurance regarding weight gain, i.e., the average client gains no weight following cognitive-behavioral therapy, the therapist must also point out that some weight gain for the underweight client may occur because the client begins to return to a biologically appropriate weight. Cognitive restructuring may have to begin earlier than usual for such clients to allow them to make progress in altering their eating patterns.

The Overweight Client

Although overweight clients with Bulimia Nervosa may not be as terri-fied of small weight gains as markedly underweight clients, they may also have unrealistic notions regarding weight loss. Because of these expectations, they run the risk of reinstating dieting with a subsequent relapse in binge eating and purging. Here the argument can be made that the cycle of dieting, binge eating, and purging has not worked to maintain weight, and has been accompanied by much misery in terms of preoccupation with food, anxiety, and guilt. The sensible alternative is to eat regularly, not to diet, and to adhere to a sensible exercise program. It has been the authors' clinical experience that such clients will tend to lose some weight if they adhere to the cognitive-behavioral therapy prescriptions, and that with cognitive restructuring they can more easily accept their body weight and shape.

Issues Regarding Weight in Binge-Eating Disorder

Clients with binge-eating disorder exhibit many similarities to overweight clients with Bulimia Nervosa. One difference is that they seek treatment later in the course of the disorder than clients with Bulimia Nervosa and are, therefore, older than clients with Bulimia Nervosa. Most binge eating clients come to the clinic seeking weight loss treatment rather than treatment for an eating disorder. It is, therefore, important to screen clients presenting for the treatment of overweight and to suggest treatment for their binge eating problems, which evidence suggests must be resolved before they have a chance to maintain their weight losses.

There are two important differences in the treatment of these clients. First, such clients will tend to gain weight during cognitive-behavioral treatment. To prevent this, some elements of a weight control program should be added to the first phase of CBT. These should include the following: weekly weighing, as is done for clients with Bulimia Nervosa, but with the aim of tracking any weight gains; the introduction of a mild exercise program and adherence to that program; and a gradual reduction of fat in the diet. These elements appear to stop substantial weight gain during the course of CBT.

Clients who stop binge eating following the completion of CBT should then continue with a behavioral weight loss program which incorporates elements of CBT. The aim is to achieve a sensible lifestyle without dietary restriction. Such a program may lead to average weight losses of some 10 to 15 pounds. It should be emphasized that these weight losses can be maintained and that clients who do not stop bingeing will continue to gain weight. Research has shown (Agras, et al., in press) that the difference between those who stop bingeing and those who continue may be as much as 16 pounds at one year post treatment. For those clients who do not stop binge eating, some alternative approaches are discussed in Chapter 12.

CHAPTER 6

Preliminary Evaluation

Before beginning treatment it is necessary to evaluate the client's complaints. This can be done either by the professional who will become the client's therapist, or by another professional who will screen the client. The format of Session 1 of cognitive-behavioral therapy will vary somewhat depending upon whether the therapist does the initial assessment of the client.

The assessment should cover three areas: the nature of the eating disorder, associated comorbid Axis I psychopathology, and comorbid Axis II psychopathology. In addition, the client should also be medically screened to investigate and, if necessary, to treat common medical conditions associated with Bulimia Nervosa such as hypokalemia and anemia.

Assessment of the Eating Disorder

Assessment of the eating disorder may either be informal, i.e., a semi-structured screening interview, or formal, e.g., using the Eating Disorder Examination developed by the Oxford group (Cooper & Fairburn, 1987). This examination is now considered the standard research and clinical instrument for the evaluation of clients with eating disorders.

The best approach is to ascertain the general nature of the eating disorder first, i.e., the presence or absence of binge eating and purging, dietary restriction, or low weight, or some combination. The approximate time course of the illness and any obvious precipitating factors should also be ascertained. Having obtained the broad picture of the eating disorder, it is important to screen out clients meeting diagnostic criteria for Anorexia Nervosa before beginning CBT. These criteria include a low body weight (BMI less than or equal to 17.5 kg/m^2); a restricted eating pattern; a distorted view of weight or shape, especially of certain body parts (e.g., stomach, thighs, arms), despite being objectively underweight; a fear of gaining weight; and, in females, absence of menstruation.

Having excluded the diagnosis of Anorexia Nervosa, attention should now be paid to the dietary pattern of the client. The therapist should first take a careful history of binge eating episodes, helping the client to classify them as "large" or "small" and then obtain an average number of large binges over the last 4 weeks. The average number of large binges is then determined for the past 3 months to ascertain if the client meets the frequency criteria for Bulimia Nervosa, or for a 6-month period to ascertain if the client meets the duration criteria for binge-eating disorder. Similarly, the pattern of purging (if any) should be examined in detail, taking a history of the various methods used both at present and in the past. These methods include: self-induced vomiting, the use of laxatives (and the type of laxative used), and the use of diuretics. The presence or absence of long periods of fasting directed toward controlling weight or shape should be ascertained. Exercise directed toward controlling weight and shape should also be examined in some detail. The type of exercise, the amount of exercise, and an estimate of how driven the exercise is should be ascertained. Dietary restriction should then be examined by having the client recall the time of eating, and the amount and type of food eaten in the last 24 hours, and inquiring about the typicality of the dietary pattern. The existence of food rules should also be determined, i.e., rules about what and when to eat. Some clients with Bulimia Nervosa defend their restricted eating pattern by portraying it as vegetarian. However, their limited choices of foods, dietary pattern (e.g., long intervals between eating), and the existence of food rules reveals the restricted nature of the food intake. The strength of concerns about weight and shape should also be determined.

Assessment of Comorbid Psychopathology

From the viewpoint of Axis I disorders, the most important conditions to evaluate are those commonly comorbid with eating disorders. These include Major Depressive Disorder, Dysthymic Disorder, the anxiety disorders, and substance dependence and abuse. The most commonly found Axis II disorders are aspects of the Cluster B personality disorders, especially Borderline Personality Disorder. As noted earlier, the two major contraindications to the treatment of Bulimia Nervosa and binge-eating disorder are the presence of a Major Depressive Episode severe enough to stop the client from fully engaging in therapy, and alcohol or drug dependence and abuse. Both of these conditions should be treated before beginning treatment of an eating disorder.

Introduction of Treatment Options

After establishing an eating disorder diagnosis that warrants cognitive-behavioral treatment and ruling out Anorexia Nervosa, the evaluator should discuss the treatment decision with the client. He or she should apprise the client of the various treatments for the disorder, explaining why cognitive-behavioral therapy is the preferred treatment. A brief description of the therapy may be helpful at this point. In addition, the assessor should determine aspects of the client's motivation, pointing out that the treatment of an eating disorder takes consider-able time and effort. The client's availability for treatment should be examined, i.e., flexibility in scheduling sessions, and any potential barriers to treatment should be explored. If the client is interested in pursuing therapy, he or she should be given the Client Workbook and asked to read Chapter 1 *An Assessment of Your Eating Problems: Is It Time to Begin Treatment?* Specific exercises provided for the client include a checklist of symptoms of the eating disorder and a listing of the pros and cons of treatment, which will help the client assess his or her need and motivation for treatment.

In the next section the first phase of cognitive-behavioral therapy is detailed. It is suggested that the therapist read both the Therapist Guide and Client Workbook before embarking on treatment.

SECTION 2

The First Phase of Cognitive-Behavioral Therapy

CHAPTER 7

The First Session

The Agenda for the First Session

- Establish a working relationship with the client
- Take a brief history of the eating disorder
- Personalize the cognitive-behavioral model of Bulimia Nervosa and binge-eating disorder for the client, gaining at least an initial acceptance of the model
- Provide a rationale for the therapy using the model
- Explain the duration and the three-phase structure of treatment
- Explain the session structure
- Provide information on the likely outcome of treatment
- Provide a rationale for self-monitoring
- Demonstrate self-monitoring
- Introduce the Client Workbook
- Assign homework

History Taking

As noted in the previous chapter, it is important that a thorough evaluation of the client be made before beginning therapy, either by the therapist or by another professional. If the assessment was made by the therapist, a portion of the first session can be devoted to recapitulating the main points covered in the previous history taking and to fleshing out any remaining details of the history that would be useful before introducing the rationale for cognitive-behavioral therapy. If the assessment was made by another professional, whose notes are presumably available to the therapist, then about half of the first session can be devoted to obtaining a history of the eating disorder and developing a working relationship with the client. The therapist will also ask about the development of the eating disorder, including its time course and any obvious events that led to its beginning. Having obtained the broad picture of the eating disorder, the therapist will ask for more details about the client's eating patterns and related attitudes, including the frequency and type of binge eating episodes (e.g., whether they are "large" or "small"), the extent of dietary restriction, the intensity and nature of the client's concerns about weight and shape, and the existence of any food rules. Similarly, the pattern of purging (if there is any) will be examined in detail, including a history and current assessment of the various methods used (e.g., vomiting, laxatives, diuretics). The client should also be asked about other issues that are sometimes related to eating disorders, including the presence or absence of depressed or anxious mood and substance use or abuse. Finally, a social and medical history will be obtained including family and other interpersonal relationships, past or present physical problems, and prior experiences in treatment. The client's level of motivation and commitment to begin and follow through with treatment at this time, and any potential obstacles to doing so should be explored. If obstacles are found, the client and therapist will spend some time discussing the pros and cons of beginning treatment at this time.

If the client decides to proceed with treatment, the remaining information gathered should be aimed at personalizing the cognitive-behavioral model for the client. It is important to cover all the agenda items for this first session thoroughly.

The Rationale for Cognitive-Behavioral Therapy

Given that dieting (usually driven by weight and shape concerns) underlies the vicious cycle of binge eating and purging, the first aim of treatment will be to help the client normalize his or her eating behavior. This includes working toward a regular pattern of eating three meals and two snacks each day by the clock. The clock is used because the normal feelings of hunger and satiety do not provide an accurate guide to food consumption in clients with eating disorders.

Clients may raise concerns at this point about potential weight gains if they follow the prescribed regimen. They should be told that this issue will be thoroughly discussed at the next session, but that in the studies published to date, on average clients gain at most a pound or two. Most of this gain is due to overcoming dehydration.

For the client with binge-eating disorder, some education regarding the link between binge eating and weight gain should be added at this time. In addition, binge eating clients should be informed that stopping binge eating is usually associated with modest weight loss, and that cognitive-behavioral therapy will include prescription of a mild exercise regimen and attention to the composition of the diet.

It should be emphasized that all changes made within the program will be gradual and that it is essential for the client to take some risks and endure the fear provoked by behaving differently. Therapy is an excellent time to experiment with new behaviors, to observe the results of those behavior changes, and to obtain feedback and guidance from the therapist.

The Duration and Three-Phase Structure of Therapy

The therapist should explain the duration and structure of therapy as detailed in Chapter 4 of this Therapist Guide. It is important for the client to understand that there is a logical progression of treatment, beginning with establishing a regular pattern of eating, followed by expanding food choices and adding feared foods in appropriate quantities to the diet. As work toward these aims progresses, the focus shifts to examining other triggers for binge eating—such as distorted thinking about food intake, weight, and shape—that may be maintaining the eating disorder. Specific triggers, such as feeling upset after a faulty interpersonal interaction, will need to be addressed in treatment. Finally, residual problems are examined, ways of coping with them are identified, and a plan is formulated for the months following treatment.

The Structure of the Session

The session structure was also outlined in Chapter 4. The therapist should explain to the client that therapy progresses optimally if sessions are well structured. Normally the session begins with the client's brief overview of trends in eating behavior, purging, and attempts to change his or her behavior. This will be followed by a more detailed examination of these issues using the client's Daily Food Record as a guide to the details of each eating episode. The therapist will then set an agenda for the remainder of the session, followed by a discussion of new changes the client should attempt and an agreement on the method the client should use. This will lead to setting a specific homework task to complete before the next session, and usually to a review of what has been accomplished during the session. The therapist should, of course, be flexible enough to alter the session structure if the client has met with a crisis or emergency during the past few days, or has particular difficulty accepting an item of the agenda. Nonetheless, in general, therapy progresses best when the agenda is set and accomplished and is consistent with the phase of therapy.

The Likely Outcome of Treatment

Using the material in Chapter 3, the therapist can provide the client with some facts regarding the likely outcome of treatment. It is important that the client know that cognitive-behavioral therapy has been tested in numerous controlled outcome studies and has been found to be the most effective approach to the treatment of Bulimia Nervosa (and binge-eating disorder) (Fairburn, Agras, & Wilson, 1992). During treatment about 50–55% of clients will completely recover, and a further 25% will show very good improvement (Fairburn, et al., 1992). Some of the latter group will completely recover over the next few months if they continue to apply the principles learned during therapy

(Agras, Rossiter, et al., 1994). Hence, there is room for considerable optimism concerning the likelihood of improvement in the client's eating disorder.

The client might also be told that the results appear to be enduring. Follow-up studies after completion of cognitive-behavioral therapy suggest that most clients maintain their improvements (Agras, Rossiter, et al., 1994; Agras, et al., in press; Fairburn, et al., 1993). There may be occasional exacerbation of symptoms, in which case the client should resume using the strategies learned during treatment, or return for a few extra therapy sessions to overcome the lapse quickly.

Self-Monitoring

The rationale for self-monitoring should now be explained to the client. The reasons for keeping detailed records of food intake, binge eating, purging, and exercise levels, as well as other aspects of eating behavior should be emphasized:

- to become more aware of the exact pattern of disturbed eating

- to provide examples of behavior for the client and therapist to consider changing

- to provide a record of the progress being made

The Daily Food Record

A new Daily Food Record should be used each day with the day of the week and date noted at the top. The *Time* column is for recording the time of each eating episode including drinks. The *Food Intake* column is for recording the type and quantity of the food or liquid consumed, not calories and fat grams. Food and beverages should be recorded immediately after they are consumed. Each meal, defined as a "separate episode of eating that was controlled, organized, and eaten in a normal fashion," should be identified with brackets ({}). Snacks and other eating episodes should not be bracketed. The *Location* column should indicate the place where the food was consumed. The *Binge* column is for noting eating episodes considered by the client to constitute a binge (*B*). The *Purge* column (for use with Bulimia Nervosa) is for recording self-induced vomiting (*V*), laxative use (*L*; note the type and amount used), or diuretics (*D*; again note the type and amount used). The *Situation* column should be used to note events that influenced eating, e.g., hunger, an argument that led to binge eating, and so on, and weight if the client weighs herself. The type and duration of exercise engaged in each day should be noted in the *Situation* column by the client with Bulimia Nervosa and in the *Exercise* section by the client with binge-eating disorder. The addition of space for recording planned exercise and the removal of the *Purge* column are the main differences in the Daily Food Record for the treatment of binge-eating disorder.

The Client Workbook

The therapist should then discuss with the client the use of the Client Workbook. The client should be told that the first four chapters cover the main elements of the first phase of treatment, and that reading one chapter after each of the first four sessions is a desirable goal. Some of the following advantages of using the Client Workbook can be pointed out:

- It gives the client time to absorb much of the educational material covered in the sessions, and also clarifies the therapeutic procedures used.

- The client can review the chapters after particular sessions, can go back and review pertinent chapters if he or she is having difficulty with a particular area, and can use the Client Workbook after treatment has been completed.

- It is also useful for some clients in educating family members about the disorder and its treatment.

Conclusion and Homework

The therapist should ask if the client has any questions about the treatment. These should either be answered fully, or touched upon briefly if they involve details that will be dealt with in later sessions. The homework for the time until the next session will be to keep accurate Daily Food Records and to read Chapters 1 and 2 of the Client Workbook (or only Chapter 2 if Chapter 1 has already been read).

CHAPTER 8

The Second Session

The Agenda for the Second Session

- Review of Daily Food Records with the aims of reinforcing and shaping accurate record keeping

- Use of data from the record, and if necessary additional history, to reinforce the cognitive-behavioral model and the rationale for therapy

- Introduction of weekly weighing

- Education about weight

- Facilitation of self-disclosure of the disorder to significant others

Review of Daily Food Records

Because the Daily Food Records kept by the client are a central aspect of therapy, it is important to pay detailed attention to them at the second therapy session. After greeting the client and asking a general question as to how things have gone since the last session, the therapist and client should go over the Daily Food Records meal by meal. Reinforcement of record keeping is accomplished by attention and importance the therapist gives to the records, and by appropriate praise for aspects of the records that have been well kept. Review of the Daily Food Records should identify any omissions and difficulties that the client may have had in keeping them. Such problems should be noted and placed on the agenda for follow-up after completing the review of the records. The Daily Food Record review should provide a detailed view of the client's eating behavior, including meals, snacks, binges, and purging. Clarification of the amounts of food consumed, if this is unclear from the record, is a useful reminder to the client regarding the accuracy of record keeping.

The final purpose of this initial review is to use the information to reinforce the relevance of the cognitive-behavioral model for the client. This can be done by looking for long periods of food deprivation followed by binge eating, and pointing out the relationship between such deprivation and binge eating. This can also help to "normalize" binge eating, by pointing out that the client is simply compensating for the previous caloric deficit by eating a large amount of food, i.e., a binge. Defining the relationship between dietary restriction and binge eating allows the therapist to repeat the rationale for working toward consuming three meals and two snacks each day.

The Daily Food Record shown in Figure 8.1 is from the first few days of self-monitoring in a client with Bulimia Nervosa. She demonstrates a very restricted pattern of eating that has long gaps between eating episodes. She reports just three eating episodes in the day, with gaps of 4.5 hours between each episode. In addition, only the lunch-time episode approximates a normal meal. In a session with this client, the therapist would emphasize the role of dietary restriction in maintaining binge eating—referring to the cognitive-behavioral model—and would note the long delays between meals. This particular client might also be encouraged to make some notes in the Situation column. Finally, a gentle nudge might be given to have her record the number of cookies that she ate at 6:30 p.m.

Tracking Binge and Purge Behaviors

The notion of tracking binge and purge behaviors should now be introduced to the client. The aim here is to add the weekly graphing of progress in reducing binge eating and purging to the homework. Chapter 3 of the Client Workbook introduces the Binge and Purge Progress Record that the client should be encouraged to fill out on a particular day each week. For the client with binge-eating disorder, only the frequency of binge eating is recorded.

Daily Food Record

Day _____   Date _____

Time	Food Intake	Location	Binge	Purge	Situation
9:30 am	(1 bowl of soup)	kitchen			
2:00 pm	(tuna sandwich)				
6:30 pm	chocolate chip cookies with coffee				

Figure 8.1. Example of a Daily Food Record for a Client With Bulimia Nervosa

Weekly Weighing and Education About Weight

Clients with Bulimia Nervosa and binge-eating disorder either weigh themselves too frequently, thus becoming demoralized over small weight gains that have no meaning, or avoid weighing themselves completely. The notion of weekly weighing should be introduced in the context of education about weight changes that might be expected during the course of treatment. The majority of studies of cognitive-behavioral therapy for Bulimia Nervosa have found either no weight gain on average, or small gains. Thus, in general one can assuage clients' fears that they are going to lose control of their weight by beginning to eat more normally. It should be noted, however, that the average may be misleading because some clients lose weight and others gain weight. The basic point is that clients will tend to move toward a more natural weight.

It should be pointed out that clients' present behavior has many costs, including constant preoccupation with food, guilt about binge eating and purging, and the effect that such behavior has on their relationships with people—whether or not they hide their behavior, as well as health consequences, such as the effects on teeth. The amount of time taken up with the disorder often isolates the client from others, leading to deteriorating interpersonal relationships. It seems reasonable to trade off these disadvantages for the risk that they may gain some weight.

The clinically overweight client may be particularly concerned about the possibility of weight gain, because such individuals may have been struggling against weight gain. The argument to make in such cases is that behavior resulting in Bulimia Nervosa has not been successful and has resulted in many negative effects. Hence, it seems reasonable to take the risk of changing his or her behavior to see what weight changes result. It might be mentioned that as treatment progresses the problem of the client's weight will not be forgotten, and that a sensible weight control program will gradually be developed should it prove necessary. It has been the authors' clinical experience that the clinically overweight client with Bulimia Nervosa tends to lose some weight when he or she stops binge eating.

The clinically underweight client may also be markedly concerned about weight gain. Many of these individuals have previously recovered from Anorexia Nervosa or are close to meeting the criteria for anorexia, and have very strong concerns about weight and shape. These clients present a difficult therapeutic problem because low weight seems to be a factor predicting a poor outcome from treatment. The pros and cons analysis—symptoms versus the risk of some weight gain—may be useful in such cases. The therapist may also remind the client that he or she is proficient in losing weight and can always return to that condition if a new weight is not tolerable. He or she should view the treatment as an experiment and commit to taking the risk of learning to live differently.

For clients with binge-eating disorder (but not clients with Bulimia Nervosa) it is suggested that they plot their weights each week on the chart shown in Figure 8.2. This will provide the longer-term feedback that is useful for these individuals in controlling their weight. This chart is not mentioned in the Client Workbook, nor is it included in the Monitoring Forms Packet, because clients with Bulimia Nervosa have the objective of lessening their concern about weight, and therefore should not record their weight changes. If the therapist chooses, Figure 8.2 may be copied for distribution to selected clients.

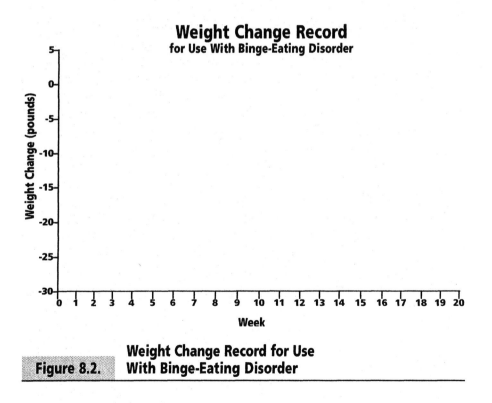

Figure 8.2. Weight Change Record for Use With Binge-Eating Disorder

Self-Disclosure

A few years ago it was usual for clients with Bulimia Nervosa to hide their binge eating and purging from everyone with whom they lived. This situation has changed somewhat with the better acceptance of eating disorders due to education by the media. However, some clients continue to hide their behaviors from everyone. Hence, it is useful to inquire as to whether the client has confided in anyone about having an eating disorder. If no disclosure has been made to significant others, e.g., a husband, the reasons for this should be explored, and some discussion of the advantages of disclosure made. Making the disorder known to those close to the client can provide extra motivation to improve because confiding makes the disorder more real. In addition, some of the burden of guilt can be relieved, as well as the necessity for deceiving those with whom the client lives by hiding the evidence of binge eating and purging.

The Client With Binge-Eating Disorder

Clients with binge-eating disorder generally range from being overweight to seriously obese. It is clear that stopping binge eating together with a sensible weight control program allows these clients to lose a little weight, but more importantly to stabilize those weight losses. Figure 8.3 shows a graph adapted from a follow-up study (Agras, et al., in press) of clients with binge-eating disorder. It may be useful for the therapist to draw this graph in rough form for the client.

A Daily Food Record for a client with binge-eating disorder is shown in Figure 8.4. This record is fairly typical for such clients, who tend to eat larger meals than clients with bulimia. However, this client has long intervals between meals, over 7 hours between lunch and dinner. When this pattern is evident in a client with binge-eating disorder, exactly the same points that were suggested for the client with Bulimia Nervosa can be made.

Homework

The homework assignment should be to begin a single weekly weighing at a regular time and to note that weight on the Daily Food Record.

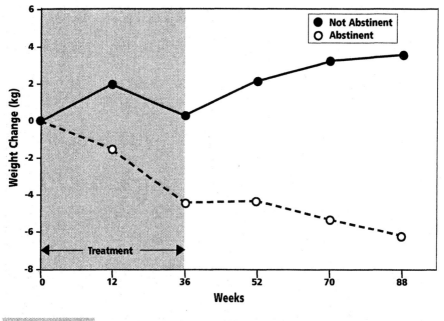

Figure 8.3.   **Weight Change in Clients With Binge-Eating Disorder**

Any changes in self-monitoring resulting from the session should form a second homework task. The therapist should encourage the client to read Chapter 3 of the Client Workbook: *Learning More About Your Pattern of Eating.*

Note that the only behavior change prescription given at this session is weekly weighing. In the next session the first prescriptions regarding eating behavior will be provided.

Daily Food Record

Day _____ Date _____

Time	Food Intake	Location	Binge	Situation
7:30 am	(Sourdough bread with peanut butter) 1 piece, 3-4 tbs. peanut butter			Breakfast
12:30 pm	(pizza)—vegetarian 2 large pieces			Lunch
8:00 pm	(Salad with ranch dressing, 1c., vegetable lasagna @ 2 cups sourdough bread—2 pcs.)			Dinner
9:30 pm	popcorn with margarine 3-4 cups, 2 tbs.		B	

Figure 8.4. **Example of a Daily Food Record for a Client With Binge-Eating Disorder**

Exercise:

10:00 am   walked 15 minutes

Overcoming Eating Disorders

Figure 8.4.   Example of a Daily Food Record for a Client With Binge-Eating Disorder (continued)

The Third Session

The Agenda for the Third Session

- Review of the client's self-monitoring

- Education regarding dietary restriction, hunger, satiety

- Education regarding the relative ineffectiveness of self-induced vomiting

- Education and prescription regarding stopping laxative use if relevant

- Prescription regarding decreasing the intervals between eating episodes

- Exercise prescription for the client with binge-eating disorder

- Homework assignments

The structure of this session should follow that outlined previously, namely, greeting the client and making a general inquiry about how things have gone since the last session, followed by a review of the Daily Food Records. The agenda is then set for the session and the topics worked through, followed by a brief recapitulation of what has been achieved, and the assigning of homework.

Review of Self-Monitoring

As in the previous session the therapist should review the Daily Food Records with the client, noting the days on which records were well kept, and also helping to correct any deficiencies in the records such as missing descriptions of quantities of food, food types, time of eating episodes, etc. Areas pertinent to the main topic of the session should be noted by the therapist for further review following agenda setting. The therapist should also begin to involve the client in the review of the self-monitoring records, for example, asking the client for his or her observations about what he or she has written. Eventually, much of the record review will be generated by the client rather than by the therapist, with the client being able to focus on the most pertinent aspects of the record.

An example of a Daily Food Record for a full day is shown in Figure 9.1. This record demonstrates both dietary restriction and long gaps between meals. For example, between 12:30 p.m. and 6:30 p.m. the client eats only three candies, a gap of 6 hours. There are no episodes of binge eating, and the amount of food eaten is clearly insufficient, leading the client to experience hunger during much of the day. This page of the record would be noted by the therapist to consider further following agenda setting. The therapist might also ask during the review of the record about the amount of popcorn eaten at 6:30 p.m., and the size of the bowl of cereal, underlining the importance of accurate monitoring of portion size.

The remainder of the session focuses on education regarding dieting, self-induced vomiting, and laxative use (if the client is using laxatives). It is often useful to explore the client's beliefs regarding these issues (particularly self-induced vomiting and laxative use) before providing corrective information.

Education Regarding Dietary Restriction, Hunger, and Satiety

Education regarding dietary restriction, hunger, and satiety sets the stage for the prescription regarding regular eating. Long-term dieting leads to several problems. First, the pattern of food intake tends to become irregular, often with long gaps between meals, or sometimes

Daily Food Record

Day _____ Date _____

Time	Food Intake	Location	Binge	Purge	Situation
8:50 am	Nonfat latte	car			hungry, rushed, running late
12:30 pm	(Veggie hot dogs, chips)	living room TV			hungry
2:00 pm	hard candy (1)	shopping			
4:30 pm	hard candies (2)	shopping			Usually eat 3, so I was still craving a third. Felt a little guilty.
6:30 pm	Popcorn Coffee—pot of decaf	TV living room			not really hungry craving popcorn
11:30 pm	Bowl of cereal	kitchen			hungry, sort of

Figure 9.1. Example of a Full Day's Daily Food Record for a Client With Bulimia Nervosa

chaotic, with numerous small eating episodes during the day. Second, dieting is associated with a restriction in the variety of food eaten, and accompanied by many rules about what to eat and what not to eat. When control breaks down the client tends to eat foods that are forbidden by dietary rules. The enjoyment of eating these foods, combined with the guilt over breaking food rules, sets up a vicious cycle of further dieting and binge eating. Third, hunger, which should normally precede a meal, tends either to be experienced almost all day (due to the caloric deficit secondary to dieting), or not experienced when it might be expected (i.e., after not eating for several hours). Fourth, because dieting, binge eating, and purging vary the size of meals, the experience of satiety becomes disrupted. Clients often experience feelings of fullness after eating only a small amount of food, or may experience fullness only after very large eating episodes. For these reasons, irregular eating patterns disturb clients' ability to rely on their internal feelings of hunger and satiety to regulate eating.

In essence, strict dieting leads to a caloric deficit for which the client's physiology tries to compensate. A large eating episode results. Such episodes (which can be viewed as normal compensation) are experienced as a binge, with all the concomitant feelings of being out of control, feeling anxious or depressed, and then guilty.

Education Regarding Self-Induced Vomiting

Self-induced vomiting provides few benefits and is associated with a number of health hazards. Nutrients, including calories, from food that is eaten are quickly absorbed from the stomach. Although many clients with Bulimia Nervosa feel that they are able to purge most of the calories that they have eaten, this is simply not true. A sizable fraction of calories consumed in a binge are, in fact, absorbed. Hence, self-induced vomiting is a somewhat inefficient method of ridding the body of calories. More-over, eating followed by purging, often followed by another binge and more purging, leads the body to give false signals regarding hunger and satiety. Hence, individuals who purge are receiving faulty feedback about their nutritional status from their bodies. Internal regulatory mechanisms then take control, "forcing" the client with Bulimia Nervosa to make up for the chronic caloric deprivation. Such eating episodes are experienced as being out of the client's control and are labeled as a binge.

This form of purging also has undesirable health consequences. Of these the most important may be dental decay because of the acid in the mouth combined with the sugars from binge food. Potassium is depleted from the body in a small proportion of clients, with undesirable consequences on cardiovascular function. In some clients, there is marked swelling of the salivary glands, giving an appearance of "mumps." Hence, there are many reasons to stop purging.

Prescription Regarding Laxative Abuse

Clients who are abusing laxatives as a form of purging should first be educated about the problems with laxative abuse. Laxative abuse is not an effective method for ridding the body of calories, indeed it is the least effective method that could be chosen. All of the caloric content of food has been absorbed by the time food is in the part of the intestinal tract that is emptied by laxatives. Laxative use leads to cycles of dehydration and rehydration with consequent aggravation of negative feelings about body shape. In addition, the use of stimulant laxatives reduces the normal contractions of the intestines, hence clients must keep on using the laxatives to avoid constipation.

The best method of treating laxative abuse is to have the client stop the laxatives abruptly, throwing away all of his or her supplies. Slowly decreasing laxative use simply prolongs the side effects of laxative withdrawal. Clients should be told that they will probably experience discomfort for 10 days to 2 weeks, including constipation, bowel discomfort and cramping, and a temporary weight gain due to rehydration. However, they should also be told that the majority of clients have relatively little trouble stopping this form of purging. Simple methods of treating constipation such as consuming additional bran, fruit, and salads, can also be suggested. For clients who refuse to quit abruptly, or have trouble following this regimen, a scheduled reduction of laxatives over a 10-day period can be tried, together with the substitution of a bulk laxative if needed. Such a schedule should be developed and individualized with the help of the client.

Prescription Regarding Regular Eating

The prescription of regular eating forms the framework for the rest of the first phase of treatment. The educational material concerning dieting, combined with a reminder about the cognitive-behavioral model, forms a useful platform from which to launch the prescription. Given that the client is experiencing abnormal sensations of hunger and fullness, the therapist should suggest that for the time being the client should eat by the clock. The eating pattern to work toward is the consumption of three meals and at least two snacks daily, with no gaps longer than 3 hours (during the waking day) between eating episodes. In the case of the client whose self-monitoring record was discussed previously (see Figure 9.1), this would mean eating something solid for breakfast at 8:50 a.m., adding a snack at about 10:00 a.m., eating lunch as she did at 12:30 p.m., then having a snack at about 3:00 p.m., and dinner at 6:30 p.m., and even possibly adding a snack before retiring. Eating between these regular snacks and meals should be eliminated, and all eating episodes should be planned.

The rationale behind this plan should be restated, i.e., that stopping dieting will eventually lead to the cessation of binge eating and purging, and that a regular eating pattern will allow retraining of normal hunger and satiety sensations. It should be noted that this change can be made gradually over the next few weeks. The therapist might discuss with the client a specific plan for the next day's food intake, including problems that might interfere with this new eating pattern and solutions to such problems.

The Client With Binge-Eating Disorder

The prescription of regular eating is as central to the client with binge-eating disorder as it is to the client with Bulimia Nervosa. In addition, a prescription for a regular exercise program should be made. Clients with binge-eating disorder tend to put on weight during cognitive-behavioral therapy, so it is important to combine some of the elements of a weight control program with cognitive-behavioral therapy. These include weekly weighing, plotting weight change on the graph, instituting a regular exercise program, and decreasing the amount of fat consumed.

Unlike clients with Bulimia Nervosa, most clients with binge-eating disorder do not exercise regularly or even at all. The first step is for the therapist to examine the frequency and duration of exercise on the client's Daily Food Record. The most promising and least costly exercise program is a brisk walk at least 30 minutes a day for at least 4 days each week. For those clients who have done no exercise, a graduated schedule should be developed jointly. For example, 10 minutes of walking at a moderate pace four times each week might suffice, or 30 minutes of moderately paced walking once or twice a week. The client should wear comfortable shoes and should begin the walking program at a time that will fit into his or her schedule and be likely to be maintained. If the client has the equipment, then a stationary bicycle, treadmill, etc., can replace the walking prescription. The goal is to develop a convenient and pleasurable exercise program that will be maintained. An occasional client will already be exercising more than the amount suggested here. Therapists should use their judgment as to whether to increase the level, or to encourage the client to continue at the same level.

Homework

Homework will include continued self-monitoring to work toward establishing a regular meal pattern, and cessation of laxative abuse where appropriate. The client should be encouraged to read Chapter 4 of the Client Workbook: *Understanding the Binge-Eating Cycle.* There are two specific exercises suggested in this chapter: identifying factors that contribute to binge eating, and identifying pleasurable alternative activities to binge eating.

For the client with binge-eating disorder the agreed-upon exercise prescription should be part of the homework assignment.

The Fourth Session

The Agenda for the Fourth Session

- Review of self-monitoring

- Work toward a regular meal pattern

- Further education if needed regarding the cognitive-behavioral model, weekly weighing, and other material not fully covered in the third session

- Dealing with any emerging compliance problems

- Assigning homework

Review of Self-Monitoring

In the fourth and subsequent sessions of the first phase of treatment the session structure should follow that outlined above. The principal focus is on the Daily Food Records. The client gradually will take the lead in reviewing records and the therapist will note items that fit the agenda, with emphasis on the pattern of eating. In the Therapist Guide, the Daily Food Records illustrating the previous sessions have shown fairly typical clients with relatively long intervals between eating episodes. The goal of treatment is to shorten these intervals with the prescription of three meals and two snacks each day.

Another pattern of eating that is encountered quite frequently is illustrated in Figure 10.1. This client has quite short intervals between eating from 8:10 a.m. to 3:00 p.m., followed by a nearly 6-hour interval until binge eating at 8:50 p.m. This illustrates two problems that have to be dealt with. First, the record is an example of a long interval between eating episodes leading to binge eating, emphasizing the importance of eating "by the clock." Second, this record from 8:10 a.m. to 3:00 p.m. illustrates a pattern that might be called grazing. In treatment such a client should be helped to begin to group the eating episodes into three meals and two snacks.

A Daily Food Record from the following week (see Figure 10.2) illustrates the client's progress toward three meals and two snacks by grouping foods previously eaten as snacks into meals. The therapist on reviewing this record would note that the apple might have been incorporated into breakfast, but would also reinforce both the grouping of items into meals and snacks and the fact that the longest gap was 4 hours.

Dealing With Adherence Problems

Problems with adherence to the treatment program are likely to emerge in the first phase of treatment and should be promptly dealt with as obstacles to progress. Among the problems are poor attendance, incomplete Daily Food Records, homework not done, failure to take risks to change, and challenging the model or prescriptions. In general, the problem needs to be directly addressed with the client, the reasons for the problem explored, and solutions generated.

Poor Attendance

Poor attendance may consist of missed sessions with only minimal warning to the therapist, missing without any warning at all, or coming late to sessions. Many clients with Bulimia Nervosa lead a somewhat disorganized life, resulting in attendance problems. Hence, it may be necessary for the therapist to explore the reasons for missing or coming late to sessions in some detail and to help the client arrive at a solution to the problem.

Another possibility is that clients with markedly avoidant personality features may feel uncomfortable in therapy. Sometimes such avoidance is accompanied by feelings that they are not meeting their perfectionistic standards, and expectations of criticism from the therapist for these

Daily Food Record

Day _____ Date _____

Time	Food Intake	Location	Binge	Purge	Situation
8:10 am	Sugar-free fruit drink—32 oz.	at desk			Weighed 125 lbs. at Don's. Didn't sleep well, so feeling tired and kind of moody; depressed. Already worried about not being able to work out today. A little hungry — felt like I should eat breakfast.
8:30 am	(Coffee w/2%nonfat milk and a little bit of hot chocolate mix Fat-free yogurt — 8 oz. 1 c. cereal)				
10:30 am	1 apple, more coffee	at desk			hungry, wanted something to eat
11:10 am	2 rice cakes (Roman Meal)	at desk			kind of hungry
1:00 pm	(A little less than 1 pint chick/ rice soup from La Costeña 1 rice cake 1/2 artichoke 2 diet sodas (24 oz. total)	at desk			Lunch time, hungry. Didn't like seeing oil in soup. Tried to eat around it. That's why I didn't eat it all. Still feel a little hungry and still feeling down.
1:40 pm	2 chocolate drops	at desk			Craving chocolate
1:50 pm	1 oz. chocolate candies (about 14)	at desk			Thought about bingeing or throwing them up but tried to talk out that it was okay. I'm feeling like I may binge later today. I'm tired.

Figure 10.1. Example of a Daily Food Record for a Client With Bulimia Nervosa Showing Grazing and a Long Interval Between Eating Episodes

3:00 pm	1 med. apple				Think I might be hungry.
8:50 pm	2 glasses red wine 4 pieces garlic bread 1 1/2 c. mixed green salad w/dressing 3 small slices roast pork 1 med. baked potato w/butter 2 bites lemon meringue pie, 1 bite cake	Mom's kitchen	B		
9:15 pm	1 piece pie 1 piece cake	in car	B		Still wanted to eat another piece and ended up eating it, deciding I would throw up after having B-day pie and cake (since I had to leave soon anyway).
9:30 pm	Dbl. scoop of ice cream	in car and in room	B	V	Thought a little about having to weigh myself in the a.m.; and felt a little nervous...wanted food out, esp. since I ate all that bread. During dinner, I thought about taking dessert home and having it later, when I was hungry, but once I felt like I ate too much bread I thought, oh well, I'll just eat it now and throw up. That way it won't be around for later.

Overcoming Eating Disorders

Figure 10.1. **Example of a Daily Food Record for a Client With Bulimia Nervosa Showing Grazing and a Long Interval Between Eating Episodes** *(continued)*

Daily Food Record

Day _____ Date _____

Time	Food Intake	Location	Binge	Purge	Situation
10:40 am	1 apple	living room			woke up at 10:30 hungry
11:00 am	{1 c. bran cereal 1/4 c. bran cereal 1/3 c. granola 1/2 banana 1 c. nonfat milk}	living room			
12:30 pm	diet soda				
1:30 pm	{French bread pizza w/light moz. cheese, mushrooms, olives, onion, and zucchini (about 2") diet soda}	back yard			Think I'm hungry — want to eat carbs cuz I plan to go on a bike ride later

Figure 10.2. Example of a Daily Food Record for a Client With Bulimia Nervosa Showing Progress Toward Regular Eating

Time	Food	Place		Thoughts/Feelings
2:55 pm	1/3 - 1/2 power bar water	living room		a little hungry, don't want to get hungry on ride Rode bike 1 1/2 hrs. hungry, tasted good
5:40 pm	1 carrot	walking around		
6:30 pm	(Rice with leftover Szechuan shrimp (about 3 c.) diet soda)	living room		hungry
7:40 pm	1 iced coffee 1 sm nonfat, sugar-free yogurt			
11:45 pm	2/3 c. cereal flakes 3/4 c. bran cereal 1/4 c. granola 3/4 c. nonfat milk	kitchen living room		Movies with Mindy. Tired, but wanted to eat something. Not hungry, but still wanted it.

Overcoming Eating Disorders

Figure 10.2.

Example of a Daily Food Record for a Client With Bulimia Nervosa Showing Progress Toward Regular Eating (continued) perceived failings. Such clients frequently arrive late or miss sessions to avoid the painful feelings evoked in therapy. It may be necessary for the therapist to identify this problem and work through it with the client, correcting erroneous beliefs about the therapy situation and the therapist's view of the client.

Finally, it may be that the client is not ready to commit enough effort for therapy to be successful. This issue can be explored by examining the pros and cons of Bulimia Nervosa (or binge-eating disorder) for him or her personally. This may help the client resolve the problem, either by deciding that he or she is not yet ready for therapy, or deciding to commit more time and effort toward therapy.

Resistance to Record Keeping

Although most clients will need some help to keep their records in a satisfactory manner, they are usually able to accomplish the task without undue difficulty. A few clients may, however, pose a greater problem, possibly stating that they are unable to keep such records. Such clients are often afraid of criticism from their therapist regarding their "bad eating behavior," about which they feel deeply ashamed. These clients are often socially phobic individuals. They are intimidated by authority figures, whom they view as critical, unpredictable persons.

A gentle but thorough exploration of these attitudes, thoughts, and feelings is important to help the client begin to resolve the problem. Educational statements pointing out that his or her disorder is common, and that he or she is no different from other clients with this problem, may be helpful. It may be necessary to shape the client's record keeping in a step-by-step manner. For example, he or she could be encouraged to keep a record for just one day, and then as he or she gained confidence this could be quickly extended.

Other clients are able to keep the records but are not willing to show them to the therapist. This can be handled at first by having the client read the records to the therapist. Again, as he or she gains confidence, sharing the written record with the therapist will be possible.

As is the case with the client who arrives late or misses sessions, it may be that failure to keep records is associated with a lack of commitment to therapy.

Failure to Comply With Behavior Change Prescriptions

It is essential that clients carry out the homework agreed upon at the end of each session. Behavior change has to take place in the client's own environment, thus it is necessary for clients to try out new behaviors, and to observe and document the results of such behavior change through self-monitoring. Failure to comply with behavior change prescriptions may stem from several causes. First, the changes agreed upon may be too difficult for the client. If this is the case, then the therapist and client need to break down the behavior changes into smaller steps and set smaller goals for homework. Second, the client may not have fully absorbed the personal implications of the cognitive-behavioral model, or some aspect of the educational efforts outlined in previous chapters. This can be remedied by outlining the model in different ways using data from the client's self-monitoring records and history to illustrate how the model specifically applies to the client. Third, the client may not be able to take the risk to change his or her behavior, fearing that the consequences such as weight gain may be catastrophic. In such a case the therapist may need to address the feared consequences specifically and in a realistic manner, at the same time pointing out that the client's present behavior is painful and damaging in many ways. Again an analysis of the perceived pros and cons of the client's disorder may be useful. It may also be useful to explore the thoughts connected with the failure to follow the prescription, and to introduce cognitive restructuring (see Chapter 16) even at this early point in therapy. Education and suggestions extending over several sessions may be needed to overcome the problem of reluctance to risk behavior changes. Therapy cannot work unless the client takes risks to make appropriate behavior changes.

The Client Who Challenges the Model or Prescriptions

One of the most difficult problems confronting a therapist is the client who continually challenges either the basic cognitive-behavioral model of Bulimia Nervosa and binge-eating disorder, or the specific interventions prescribed by the therapist. Such resistance is often diminished when the client fully trusts the therapist. Such clients often have comorbid personality disorders which contribute to their confrontational interpersonal style. Such a client may be engaged in a difficult relationship, against which he or she is rebelling or that provokes anger. One method is to take a low-key approach to the client, refusing to become engaged with the rebellious behavior. Often such clients will become less defensive when they perceive that the therapist is not hostile and can be trusted. If further education and suggestion do not help to ameliorate this behavior, it will be necessary for the therapist to confront the client's behavior directly. At this point it may be useful to explore briefly the nature of the client's current interpersonal situation. The therapist can then point out the repeated pattern of challenges made by the client, how this behavior is also evidenced in his or her everyday life, and how this behavior retards progress in therapy.

The Client With Binge-Eating Disorder

The main additions to the program for treating the client with binge-eating disorder are monitoring and extending a sensible exercise program and beginning to point out items from the Daily Food Records where the consumption of fatty foods might be reduced. These changes should be gradually introduced.

A Daily Food Record from a client with binge-eating disorder is shown in Figure 10.3. This record illustrates disordered eating behavior similar to that shown for the client with Bulimia Nervosa described previously (see Figure 10.1), and is a common pattern in binge-eating disorder. The client has frequent and disorganized eating episodes throughout the day, with an episode that begins as a snack and turns into a binge. Apart from the binge the client eats two meals and five snacks.

The type of educational procedures outlined for the client with Bulimia Nervosa described previously are clearly useful in this type of case. The client should consider beginning to eat by the clock, with three planned meals and two snacks. The procedure of planning meals and snacks for each day ahead of time is useful for this type of client. The therapist can take some time to help the client plan the next day's meals and snacks and encourage the client to do so on one or two more occasions during the next week. Praise for appropriate exercise should be given.

Homework

Homework will include continued self-monitoring, working on the specific behavior changes, and reading Chapter 5 of the Client Workbook: *New Ways of Thinking About Weight*. The therapist should refer to the Client Workbook to review specific homework assignments.

Daily Food Record

Day _____ Date _____

Time	Food Intake	Location	Binge	Situation
7:00 am	1 bran cereal, nonfat milk 1 banana 2 c. coffee)	kitchen		breakfast
9:00 am	wheat toast, honey, 2 slices	kitchen		
10:30 am	pumpkin pie, 3" round	farmer's market		snack
11:15 am	1veggie burger, lettuce, tom. dark bread bun small potato chips iced tea)	dining room	B	
11:45 am	popcorn diet soda, 8 oz.	sitting in front of TV		
2:00 pm	turkey sandwich, whole wheat bread cranberry sauce coffee/cream	kitchen		

Figure 10.3. Example of a Daily Food Record for a Client With Binge-Eating Disorder Showing Eating Patterns Similar to Bulimia Nervosa

Time	Food	Location
6:00 pm	cinnamon roll (whole wheat with honey) one large frozen yogurt	car
8:00 pm	tortilla chips (baked) bean dip (nonfat) diet soda	bedroom
9:30 pm	bagel with cream cheese	kitchen

Exercise:

10:00 am	walked 20 minutes	

Overcoming Eating Disorders

Figure 10.3. Example of a Daily Food Record for a Client With Binge-Eating Disorder Showing Eating Patterns Similar to Bulimia Nervosa (continued)

CHAPTER 11

The Remainder of Phase 1 (Sessions 5–9)

The primary focus of this phase of treatment continues to be on the restructuring of the pattern of eating, shaping the client toward eating "by the clock" (i.e., at regular, planned times), and eating three meals and two snacks each day. In addition, some restructuring of the eating episodes themselves may be necessary. For example, the Daily Food Record shown in Figure 9.1 was from a client whose breakfast consisted of only a latte coffee, and for dinner she ate popcorn and coffee. Such clients need to be engaged in a discussion about the alternative breakfast and dinner foods that they might eat. During this phase of treatment, it is not necessary to incorporate feared foods into the diet, but the client should begin to add non-feared foods and to make a clear distinction between meals and snacks. As the sessions continue the client should be encouraged gradually to increase portion sizes of meals to avoid the sensations of hunger that many clients with Bulimia Nervosa report.

An example of early restructuring of meals is shown in a record from the highly restricted client whose record from the second session was shown in Figure 8.1. In a Daily Food Record from the fourth session of treatment she is beginning to eat more frequently, although in an extremely restricted fashion (see Figure 11.1). A suitable prescription for this client would be to add something mid-morning, and to begin to differentiate meals from snacks by adding more food items to the meals. This client would probably be quite resistant to such notions, having lost 2 pounds, but should be encouraged to take risks in changing

Daily Food Record

Day _____ Date _____

Time	Food Intake	Location	Binge	Purge	Situation
10:00 am	chocolate coffee	school			145 — lost 2 pounds happy, feel in control
1:30 pm	nonfat yogurt	school			
3:15 pm	cereal coffee	school			
6:00 pm	frozen yogurt	car			
6:45 pm	1 c. soup rice, chicken chocolate	home	B	✓	

Figure 11.1. Example of a Daily Food Record for a Client With Bulimia Nervosa Showing Progress in Restrictive Eating Patterns

her behavior, because such changes are essential to recovery. Reference to the cognitive-behavioral model may also be useful in demonstrating the effects of restrictive dieting.

A quite different record is from the client whose Daily Food Record was shown in the previous chapter (see Figure 10.1), a bulimic client with strong similarities to clients with binge-eating disorder. This client is beginning to organize her eating into meals and snacks, a record that looks a good deal better than her previous week's record. Discussion in this case would center on the need to plan meals and snacks better, with the client and therapist jointly planning a typical weekend and a typical workday's eating plan.

An example of a Daily Food Record with a somewhat better structure from Session 8 of therapy for a client with Bulimia Nervosa is shown in Figure 11.2. Here, the meals can be differentiated from snacks, and the client is eating three meals and two snacks regularly. The client still demonstrates evidence of restricted eating in terms of the meal content, but this can be improved in Phase 2 of the therapy.

Meal Planning

Some clients with either Bulimia Nervosa or binge-eating disorder are able to restructure their eating patterns with little specific assistance, but others need to learn to plan their eating episodes at specific times, often with different plans for different days of the week, e.g., a workday, weekends, or any day in which the client's schedule is different. To help the client plan the timing of eating, and the content of meals and snacks, it is necessary for the therapist to understand the details of the client's daily schedule, helping him or her assess the feasibility of proposed changes. Such changes should be regarded as experimental and refined as their success or failure becomes apparent. When an overall plan has been devised, the client should be encouraged to put it in place. This may necessitate an incremental approach, beginning to use the plan on one or two days a week and gradually increasing the frequency. Other clients may be able to institute such plans more quickly. If a plan has been agreed upon, it becomes part of the homework to be accomplished between sessions, and progress in implementing the plan should be examined at the next session.

Daily Food Record

Day _____ Date _____

Time	Food Intake	Location	Binge	Purge	Situation
7:45 am	{1 bowl cereal}	home			hungry
10:30 am	1 fruit tart 2 brownies	home			snack time hungry, ate only 1 fruit tart, but 2 brownies
1:45 pm	{8 gyoza (1 serving) 1 piece of cheddar cheese}	home			Woke up after nap craving cheese. Need to cut down on high-fat foods.
4:15 pm	granola bar				snack time
6:45 pm	{tortellini can/peas}				dinner and a little hungry, trying to keep fat to a minimum

Figure 11.2. Example of a Daily Food Record for a Client With Bulimia Nervosa Showing Regular Eating Patterns

Eating Style

An examination of the client's eating style may be useful during this phase of treatment. The topic can be introduced by examining comments in the Situation column on the Daily Food Record. For example, a client may note that she ate ice cream while standing up. Further questions may reveal that she simply took the package out of the refrigerator and began to eat directly from it. This might lead to an examination of the manner and place in which all snacks and meals are consumed, with the rationale that paying attention to the context of eating may enhance self-control. Clients will often eat breakfast or snacks in the car, and they may binge under specific circumstances—such as standing up in the kitchen, watching television, and so on. It should be pointed out that by eating in a variety of places or in particular ways, those places become cues to eat. Hence, if one eats in the car, simply getting into the car may precipitate an urge to eat. The goal is to reduce the number of places in which food is consumed, working toward containing all eating episodes into a few places. Meals should be consumed sitting down at a table that has been prepared for a meal. This topic fits well with the introduction of meal planning.

Pleasurable Alternative Activities to Binge Eating and Purging

During this phase of treatment it is often helpful to have the client devise activities that are incompatible with binge eating to use when resisting urges to induce vomiting, particularly when binges are of the subjective type. During this phase objective binge episodes may disappear, leaving only subjective binges. Such binges, however, are often accompanied by uncomfortable feelings, perceived by the client as being overly full, leading to purging.

The therapist should encourage the client to consider activities that are incompatible with binge eating and purging, eventually having a list of such activities to put into use. For example, when faced with an urge to binge, the client might leave the environment in which the urge has occurred, go for a walk, call a friend, engage in some distracting activity, and so on. It should be noted that clients often choose alternative activities that are not particularly pleasant. Such alternatives would not be very useful over the long run. Hence, it is important for the therapist to urge the client to identify activities that are both pleasurable and incompatible with binge eating and purging. The therapist, for example, might get the client to list such activities and then rank them for pleasurability.

The Duration and Outcome of Phase 1

On average the first phase of this treatment program spans the first 8 weeks of therapy. The phase may be shortened for clients who rapidly alter their eating patterns and whose binge eating and purging decline, or may be lengthened for clients who are slow to adopt regular patterns of eating. Figure 11.3 shows the change in purging for six clients who recovered from Bulimia Nervosa over the 20 weeks of treatment. As can be seen, most of these clients demonstrated considerable improvement over the first 8 weeks of treatment, although the courses that they followed were quite different from one another. For example, client 4, who began by purging 19 times each week, stopped purging by week 4 (Session 6) and stayed abstinent thereafter. On the other hand, client 3 followed a somewhat bumpy course, not achieving abstinence until week 16 of treatment. On average, however, one can expect considerable reductions in binge eating and purging during the first 10 sessions of treatment. Such changes should, of course, be accompanied by changes in the pattern of eating, and reduction in dietary restraint by enlarging the size of meals in the case of the client with Bulimia Nervosa.

A similar rate of improvement should be expected for clients with binge-eating disorder. In addition to maintaining a regular pattern of meals and snacks, such clients should also be cutting down slowly on high-calorie foods, eating more appropriate foods at each meal (no leftover cake or desserts for breakfast), and increasing a regular exercise program.

Frequently Encountered Therapist Problems

Not all of the problems encountered in therapy stem from the client. The therapist may also contribute to the difficulties. Perhaps the most frequent problem is the lack of therapist adherence to the structure of the sessions. As a reminder, sessions should be structured as follows: after greeting the client and making a general inquiry about how things have gone since the last session, the Daily Food Records and any homework assigned at the last session should be reviewed. The agenda for the session should then be assigned and the topics worked

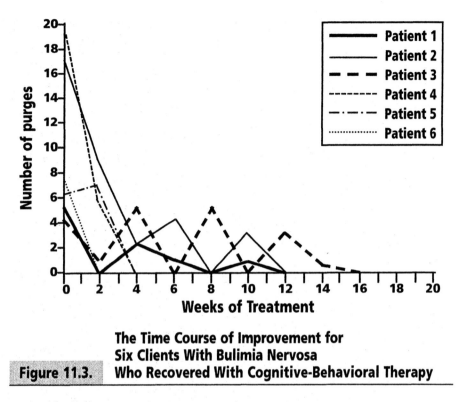

Figure 11.3. The Time Course of Improvement for Six Clients With Bulimia Nervosa Who Recovered With Cognitive-Behavioral Therapy

Note: From data collected by the authors.

through in detail, followed by a brief recapitulation of what has been achieved, and the assigning of homework to be completed before the next session. Sessions that are not structured in this manner tend to become disorganized and are unsatisfactory to both therapist and client. In addition, less progress is made in the poorly structured session.

A second problem, sometimes contributing to a poorly structured session, is the therapist's jumping at the first issue presented in the session, and examining that issue in detail, before examining the broader picture of the interval between sessions. This tendency can be avoided by adhering to the session structure, and developing an agenda for the session. The first issue may or may not appear on the agenda. Very often such issues are found to be irrelevant once the larger picture has been obtained.

Another problem is focusing too early in Phase 1 on the content of what the client eats rather than on the patterning of meals and snacks. Although it is important for both clients with Bulimia Nervosa and those with binge-eating disorder eventually to consider the introduction of feared and avoided foods, it is first necessary to help clients structure their eating patterns. Once this is accomplished and binge eating is reduced in frequency, meal content can be addressed. Another problem is allowing the client to become too passive in the therapy session. Wherever possible clients should be made to do the work. For example, rather than the therapist taking the lead in reviewing the cognitive-behavioral model, the therapist might ask the client how he or she sees his or her problem fitting into the model. This will necessitate the client's reviewing the model, aided where necessary by the therapist.

A final problem is that of extending a session when the client is late. The therapist should probably always resist such an impulse. It is, of course, necessary to examine the reason for the client's late attendance, and to problem solve so as to avoid a repetition. However, the consequence of lateness should be a shorter session, which brings home to the client the importance of being on time.

In the remaining sessions of Phase 1, the client should read Chapter 6 of the Client Workbook: *Medical Consequences of Bulimia and Binge-Eating Disorder,* and should be encouraged to review particular chapters to aid therapy progress. When the therapist is considering moving on to Phase 2 of the therapy, the client should be asked to read Chapter 7 of the Client Workbook: *Measuring Your Progress: Refining or Revising Your Strategy.* The client's attention should be drawn to the two exercises in this chapter, namely, the Midtreatment Therapy Progress Worksheet, and the Summary of Midtreatment Progress. These exercises form the basis for the evaluation of progress in Phase 1 of treatment.

CHAPTER 12

Assessing Progress

Toward the end of Phase 1 of treatment, or earlier if the situation warrants it, the therapist should assess the client's progress. If binge eating and purging fail to decline as expected, progress is not satisfactory. Some decline should be expected in this phase. If binge eating and purging have failed to decline, the therapist should review the client's self-monitoring records to determine if the client made progress toward the main goals of Phase 1: to regularize eating patterns and to lessen overall dietary restriction. This review should lead to the identification of residual problems in achieving these goals. These problems should be discussed with the client, with the goal of finding solutions. Such problems should form the first priority in the next phase of treatment. The procedures introduced in Phase 2, such as problem solving, introducing feared foods, cognitive restructuring, identifying and dealing with emotional and interpersonal binge triggers, and distorted perceptions regarding weight and shape, may be helpful in ameliorating some of the residual problems in achieving a regular and less restricted pattern of eating.

If the client has not made suitable progress, the problem areas that are outlined in this chapter might be considered. It should be noted, however, that we do not recommend combining another psychotherapeutic approach with cognitive-behavioral therapy. If the therapist decides that continuing cognitive-behavioral therapy is not appropriate, then a complete change to a new treatment is recommended. Adding another form of psychotherapeutic treatment to cognitive-behavioral therapy blurs the focus of treatment and weakens its effectiveness.

Some Reasons for Lack of Progress

Controlled treatment studies of cognitive-behavioral therapy for Bulimia Nervosa and binge-eating disorder suggest that some 10–15% of participants will drop out of therapy (Agras, 1993). Most of these dropouts occur during Phase 1 of treatment and many of them involve changes in the client's life circumstances incompatible with the continuation of therapy, for example, a change of jobs, financial problems, and transportation difficulties. Some of these problems can be avoided by a careful assessment of the client's motivation before beginning treatment, looking particularly at whether clients are being realistic about the time and effort involved in such treatment. Personality characteristics common in clients who leave treatment include marked impulsivity or major interpersonal problems. If such problems are identified early in treatment or before treatment begins, the therapist may decide to use an alternative approach to treatment such as interpersonal psychotherapy.

Apart from the dropouts from treatment, there appear to be four main problem areas for clients who do not do well in therapy:

1. Severe dietary restriction in clients with past histories of Anorexia Nervosa and strong fears of weight gain

2. Interpersonal problems, which interfere with the client-therapist relationship. For example, a client locked in a struggle with a parent in making the transition to independence may demonstrate similar behavior toward the therapist, perhaps challenging the CBT model, showing poor compliance with self-monitoring, and so on. If a straightforward confrontation concerning this issue does not improve the situation, then a switch to interpersonal psychotherapy may be desirable.

3. The emergence or deepening of depressive symptomatology or, less frequently, the emergence or aggravation of an anxiety disorder such as Panic Disorder. Both of these disorders demonstrate high rates of comorbidity with the eating disorders. Medication treatment for either condition may allow continuation of cognitive-behavioral therapy for the eating disorder once the symptoms of depression or panic have abated.

4. Impulsivity as part of a personality disorder which interferes with treatment. This may require direct confrontation by the therapist when the impulsivity interferes with the course of therapy. Careful limit setting may be helpful.

What to Do About Lack of Progress

If there has been little progress in reducing binge eating and purging, little change in restructuring the pattern of eating, combined with some increase in caloric restriction, then it is unlikely that cognitive-behavioral therapy will be helpful for this client. Unfortunately, controlled treatment research has not yet advanced to the point where the authors can give sound advice to therapists as to how to proceed in such cases, i.e., second-level treatments for clients who have made little progress in the first phase of CBT have not been addressed systematically. The available options are outlined below.

Add Antidepressant Medication

As noted in Chapter 3, antidepressants—both the tricyclic (e.g., imipramine, desipramine) compounds, and the serotonin reuptake inhibitors (e.g., fluoxetine)—have been found to be effective in the treatment of Bulimia Nervosa and binge-eating disorder. One option is, therefore, to add an antidepressant to cognitive-behavioral therapy. This addition to treatment is particularly indicated with coexistence of a Major Depressive Disorder or the emergence of panic attacks.

Change to Interpersonal Psychotherapy

For clients whose interpersonal problems appear to be interfering with progress, it may be reasonable to change the therapeutic procedure to interpersonal psychotherapy in its adaptation to eating disorders (see Chapter 3). This allows exploration of the relationship between interpersonal problems and the eating disorder, and for the resolution of such problems. Interpersonal psychotherapy may be particularly appropriate for clients with transient negative moods, and for whom binge eating ameliorates such moods. In such cases the binges may be too reinforcing for the client to give up without attention to the sources of the negative moods. As noted in Chapter 3, interpersonal psychotherapy appears to be as effective as cognitive-behavioral therapy in the treatment of both Bulimia Nervosa and binge-eating disorder (Fairburn, et al., 1991;

Fairburn, et al., 1993; Wilfley, et al., 1993), although few comparisons have been published to date.

Poor Compliance

In the previous chapter, several areas underlying poor compliance were outlined. In the case of clients who are not improving with cognitive-behavioral therapy, the therapist should revisit these potential problems and, if one is identified, should attempt to deal with the problem. This may mean pointing out the lack of progress to the client, clearly identifying the compliance problem, and pointing out to the client that without compliance to treatment success is unlikely. It is useful to attempt to identify the barriers that the client has encountered in his or her attempts to change his or her behavior. If such barriers are identified, for example, faulty cognitions or difficult life circumstances, then these barriers can become the focus of treatment.

When Progress Is Satisfactory

If the client is making reasonable progress—as indicated by a decline in binge eating and purging accompanied by appropriate dietary changes—the client should be told that he or she is making progress toward overcoming the problem. In the second phase, the goal of treatment will be to address triggers to binge eating other than dietary restriction, although as noted earlier most clients will need some further attention paid to dietary restriction in the second phase of treatment. The additional triggers include feared foods, faulty thinking, rigid food rules, interpersonal upset, and weight and shape concerns. During the last few sessions of Phase 1 the client should have been listing the circumstances in which binge eating has occurred on the Daily Food Record. The therapist can use these circumstances for future reference, because they often consist of binge triggers. If the client has not been listing such circumstances he or she should now be encouraged to do so in preparation for Phase 2. It may be useful for the therapist to explore with the client the particular events, internal or external, that trigger binge eating. This will allow the therapist and client to address the most salient issues in the second phase of treatment.

The Second Phase of Cognitive-Behavioral Therapy

CHAPTER 13

Introduction to Phase 2

The transition from the first to the second phase of treatment may begin around Session 10, but may occur earlier for clients who make rapid progress toward the goals of Phase 1, namely, structuring a regular pattern of eating with some increase in the caloric content of meals, weekly weighing, and ceasing to use laxatives. For the client with binge-eating disorder the goals of Phase 1 also include establishment of a regular exercise program, beginning to decrease the consumption of high-calorie foods, and the gradual adoption of a heart-healthy diet.

The second phase of treatment usually spans some seven or eight sessions (approximately Sessions 10–17). A primary goal of the second phase of treatment is to continue to monitor and maintain a regular pattern of eating. For the client with binge-eating disorder, the goal includes a regular exercise program and continued decrease in the consumption of high-calorie foods. The therapist should never lose sight of this goal, even when dealing with new issues in this and the next phase of therapy. The next goal, which will be explored further in Chapter 14, is to help the client delineate the nature of feared and avoided foods, and to reintroduce some of these foods into the diet gradually. In addition to continuing to address dietary triggers for binge eating, e.g., dietary restriction and avoidance of different types of food, the therapist should continue to assess other types of binge triggers experienced by the client, e.g., breaking a food or dietary rule, concerns about weight and shape, and negative affect.

The therapist then introduces a range of new procedures to the client. Although these are presented in a particular sequence in this Therapist Guide—the preferred sequence—the therapist may wish to introduce them in a different sequence or with a different emphasis, depending on the specific problems posed by the client. Following the introduction of feared foods, formal problem solving is introduced. The next procedure delineates the client's erroneous beliefs about food, shape, and weight, and challenges such beliefs using formal cognitive restructuring. Specific triggers to binge eating, whether they are related to dietary concerns, particular situations, or negative affect deriving from interpersonal interactions, are then explored. Finally, attitudes toward weight and shape are investigated, and for some clients specific behavior change exercises may be planned.

It should be noted that the session structure for this phase remains unchanged, namely first examining Daily Food Records and checking on specific homework assignments, then outlining the agenda based on this examination and the progress of therapy, working through the agenda, recapping the session, and setting homework.

Feared Foods

Feared, Avoided, and Problem Foods

An aspect of dietary restriction that is not addressed in Phase 1 of treatment is the extent to which the client avoids feared foods. In Phase 1, the primary emphasis is upon the patterning of food intake, with a gradual increase in the amount of food eaten for the restrictive client, and a gradual decrease in high-calorie foods for the binge eater. Feared and avoided foods often trigger binge eating, are eaten during binges, and may be regarded as fattening, high calorie, or high in fat content by the client.

Frequently the client will have a rule concerning such foods, such as they are bad, fattening, and should never be eaten. The client's Daily Food Records will usually reveal that the client is avoiding particular foods. This allows the therapist to put the issue of feared foods on the agenda and to encourage the client to talk about the foods that are feared or on the "bad foods" list. The history of such avoidances, their nature, and the reasons for such avoidance should be explored.

Some education regarding the issue of avoiding foods may be useful at this point. First, avoidance of anything that is feared will strengthen the fear. The only way to overcome a problem is to face it. Second, many, if not all, of the feared foods are inherently enjoyable. By avoiding such foods, individuals are setting themselves up to feel deprived, and are thereby increasing the attractiveness of such foods. This often results in the purchase of such foods and the triggering of a binge.

Method for Dealing With Feared Foods

There are two steps regarding feared foods. The first is to have the client identify the range of such foods. One way to achieve this aim is to have the client visit a supermarket and write down all foods that are regularly avoided, that cause anxiety, or that are on the "forbidden foods" list. As homework, the client should be asked to separate these foods into four categories, from the least feared in Category 1, to the most feared in Category 4. A typical list is shown in Figure 14.1.

This is preparation for the next session, which suggests that the client begin to introduce small quantities of feared foods into his or her everyday diet. The first foods to be introduced should be from the least-feared category, and the client should be encouraged to introduce one or two of these foods into the diet during the next week. Progress toward this goal should be monitored, and new items introduced in subsequent weeks. The reintroduction of feared foods becomes a new theme running through several sessions of the second phase of treatment, with the principal aim of continuing to reduce dietary restriction.

It should be pointed out to the client that he or she is not expected to eat all of these foods regularly, but that he or she should no longer feel deprived of particular foods or regard them fearfully. Some clients fear that consuming such foods will lead to weight gain. This is irrational, because eating small or even moderate amounts of a particular food will not influence weight. Moreover, clients must begin to trust their bodies to regulate their food intake.

The Client With Binge-Eating Disorder

The client with binge-eating disorder may or may not agree that feared foods exist, because many of these clients do eat such foods at mealtimes. In such cases the supermarket list should include both feared foods and high-calorie "problem" foods which may be eaten with guilt or anxiety. The goal here is to enhance the consumption of feared foods and to reduce their power as triggers for binge eating.

Feared and Problem Foods List

1	**2**	**3**	**4**
Least Avoided			**Most Avoided**

Category 1	Category 2	Category 3	Category 4
french fries	corn dogs	all pastries	all candy bars
hamburger	white milk	chocolate syrups	all ice cream
mayonnaise	chocolate milk	avocados	all rich desserts,
pizza	cheese	creamed soups	e.g., crème pies,
sugary drinks	sour cream		éclairs
canned pastas, e.g.,	nuts		bacon
ravioli, spag.	fried, frozen,		butter
chili	battered foods		liver sausage
salami	bologna		
whipped cream	cake and frostings		
rich cookies, i.e.,	ham		
crème-filled,			
chocolate-			
covered			

Figure 14.1. Example Feared and Problem Foods List

Homework

The client should read Chapter 8 of the Client Workbook: *Feared, Avoided, and Problem Foods*, and complete Exercise 8.1, Identifying Feared Foods, which includes the Feared and Problem Foods List. It may also be useful for the client to read Chapter 9: *Understanding Binge Triggers*, which introduces the reasons for the use of the procedures to be introduced in this phase of treatment. The purpose of the two exercises in Chapter 9 is getting the client to begin to list typical remaining binge triggers.

Problem Solving

Problem solving is covered in Chapter 10 of the Client Workbook. Using the Problem Solving form on the back of the Daily Food Record, clients may work through complex problems that involve multiple binge triggers. Clients should be told that it is not sufficient to do this mentally; it is a written task.

Identifying the Problem

The first challenge in problem solving is writing down a specific problem. For example, in the Client Workbook the client describes the following problem: "Because I'm in a bad mood and feel horrible about myself the only way to deal with these feelings is to binge on chocolate." Here the problem is that binge eating is perceived as the only way to deal with a bad mood. Clients often have difficulty identifying the specific problem and may need some help from the therapist to clarify the problem.

Listing Alternative Solutions to the Problem

When listing alternative solutions, the client should be encouraged to "brainstorm" to formulate as many different solutions to the problem as possible without regard to their practicality. The important aspects of this step are to make sure that the client really thinks out the various alternatives, and to ensure that the client does not prematurely rule out potentially viable solutions. This may be difficult for many clients because they have rigid ways of dealing with problem situations. At times the therapist might suggest an alternative behavior if it seems fairly obvious, simply to enlarge the list of choices. It should be noted that binge eating and purging may appear in the client's list of solutions. It is important to allow the client to consider the practicality and effectiveness of binge eating and purging together with the other solutions listed. Doing so may lead to a productive analysis of the pros and cons of binge eating and purging.

In the example given in the Client Workbook, seven alternatives are listed, including:

- "allow myself to eat some chocolate without losing control"

- "eat one portion of a chocolate dessert in a restaurant"

- "get out of the situation—go for a drive, go to gym, etc."

- "call a friend"

Evaluating Each Potential Solution for Its Practicality and Likely Effectiveness

At this stage the client should take each item on the list and consider how practical the solution is, and how effective it would be. Examples from the client follow:

- "allow myself to eat some chocolate without losing control"

  Practicality: "Don't think I can even open a box of candy without losing control and bingeing"

  Effectiveness: "Won't be effective for reason stated"

- "eat one portion of a chocolate dessert in a restaurant"

  Practicality: "Many cafes are open at this hour and I don't have a problem going out alone"

  Effectiveness: "This may work if I go to a place that offers desserts that I like and that has an atmosphere in which I can also relax and feel comfortable..."

- "get out of the situation—go for a drive, go to gym, etc."

    Practicality: "Easy to drive somewhere to delay immediate self-destructive behavior"

    Effectiveness: "Would need to combine this with another strategy"

- "call a friend"

    Practicality: "Have a few people that I could call. But they may not be home or in the mood to talk with me..."

    Effectiveness: "If the conditions are right, might be helpful, but hard to know in advance if I can rely on other people to make me feel better tonight"

Choosing One or More Solutions to the Problem Based on the Evaluation

The most feasible alternative appears to be to leave the situation and eat a portion of dessert in a restaurant. If the client had already been exposed to cognitive restructuring she could also take a pen and paper or a Problem Solving form to the restaurant and work out challenges to the problem thinking that triggered the binge.

Following Through on the Solution

To follow through, it is necessary for the client to inform the therapist each time he or she uses this particular method to solve a problem, and for the therapist to follow up by asking the client about the problem and solution in future sessions. If the client does not follow through with the identified solutions, the therapist should inquire about this and may need to encourage the client to use the Problem Solving form to overcome his or her lack of follow-through.

Reevaluating the Problem and Solutions

After implementing the solution, the client should consider the degree of success associated with the solution and if necessary revisit the problem-solving procedure to fine tune the process, or to find other solutions.

For example, some clients may not be able to brainstorm alternative solutions due to premature screening of alternatives—often because they believe every solution must be perfect. Other clients may have difficulty evaluating and selecting a solution.

Homework

The client should read Chapter 10 of the Client Workbook: *Solving Problems,* and complete a Problem Solving form as indicated in Exercise 10.1.

CHAPTER 16

Cognitive Restructuring

One of the most common triggers of binge eating is distorted thinking about a variety of issues. Most clients are not aware of the thoughts that lead to binge eating and experience the whole process as automatic. Hence, clients should be encouraged to explore the nature of their thinking that leads to binge eating. Clients vary in their ability to assess their thinking, but can usually do so with some help from the therapist. It is also helpful for the therapist to educate clients about their thought processes, pointing out that although it may not seem to be the case, they have a considerable degree of control over their thoughts, should be able to detect thoughts that lead to binges, and with the help of the therapist they can learn to challenge and correct faulty thinking. When beginning this exploration clients may confuse feelings with thoughts, so the therapist needs to help clients make the distinction. At the same time, clients should learn to pay attention to thoughts linked to strong feelings, because these salient "thought-feelings" may represent "hot" cognitions that trigger binge eating. As clients begin to identify the thoughts that trigger binge eating, they should be encouraged to identify the core aspect of a thought. The therapist should then teach them the method of evaluating the reality of a particular thought, with the goal of changing such thinking and the behavior that is related to it.

Types of Distorted Thinking

Distorted thinking usually falls into one of the five categories that follow, although the categories overlap with one another:

1. **All-or-nothing thinking.** This type of thinking is particularly common in both Bulimia Nervosa and binge-eating disorder. The client thinks in extremes, e.g., "Either I am on a diet or I am out of control." This type of thinking is often combined with perfectionism, the setting of overly high standards, e.g., "Unless I come in every week with no binge episodes I am a failure."

2. **Overgeneralization.** This consists of making an erroneous conclusion about general performance, or a series of unrelated events, based on a single negative experience, e.g., "I gained 2 pounds this week so I know that I will keep on gaining weight at that rate," or "I binged on potato chips once, so I must never again eat potato chips." Such thinking underlies the rigid rules governing food consumption that many clients with Bulimia Nervosa create.

3. **Magnifying negatives and minimizing positives.** This is also a very common distortion for clients with Bulimia Nervosa, and one to which the therapist should be alert. The client may come to the session reporting that she has had a terrible week. However, when the Daily Food Records are examined, they show that the client binged only once during the week, that the binge was subjective, and that she did not purge. In such instances the client is ignoring positive behaviors and focusing on her negative behaviors. A similar example might be a client who comes in very upset because someone made a deleterious remark about her appearance. It turns out that the remark was made by a friend who is jealous of her, and that there were several times when she was complimented on her appearance during the same week. The therapist should watch for this type of behavior during all the phases of cognitive-behavioral therapy. The client can be helped to overcome this selective distortion by exploring the positive gains and experiences that have occurred since the last session.

4. **Catastrophizing.** Here the client overestimates the negative consequences of a particular event, e.g., "If I gain 5 pounds everyone will notice. They will think that I am unattractive, and I will be rejected." Again, this distortion is frequently encountered in the client who has Bulimia Nervosa.

5. **Selective abstraction.** In this distortion, the client bases a conclusion on isolated details while ignoring contradictory and often more salient evidence, e.g., "No one talked to me at the party, so it must be because they think I'm fat and ugly." The example of cognitive restructuring narrated below deals with such a thought.

Correcting Cognitive Distortions

The client should be taught the formal method of exploring and correcting distorted thinking. Once the client has mastered the method in session, he or she should be encouraged to practice using it to identify and correct thoughts as they occur. At first he or she should delineate one or two such thoughts during the week between sessions, using the Challenging Problem Thoughts form on the back of the Daily Food Record. The process occurs in five steps, illustrated here with a dialog between the therapist and client.

Step 1. Identify the Problem Thought

T: Did you notice any situations leading to binge episodes or to urges to binge in the past week that involve problem thoughts?

C: Well, I binged after skiing one day. I was upset, because I went skiing and people were nicer to my friend than they were to me and I was sure that it was because she is thinner and prettier than I am.

T: I'm hearing some faulty reasoning here. Let's work to uncover the underlying problem thought.

C: My friend is prettier than I am, so that means that people like her more and like me less, and she's thinner. So I guess the underlying problem thought is that people don't like me because I'm fat and ugly. (At this point the therapist should have the client write down the problem thought on a copy of the form.)

Step 2. List Objective Evidence to Support

T: What is the evidence to support the view that people don't like you because you are fat and ugly?

C: Well, I am fat and ugly.

T: I think you know that is subjective, not objective.

C: OK. Objectively, my friend is more attractive than I am.

T: Let's accept that for now and write it down.

C: I was not looking my best that day.

T: Again a stretch, but we'll accept that for now. (Client writes it down). Are there others?

C: More people talked to her than to me.

T: OK. Let's go with those.

Step 3. List Objective Evidence to Dispute

T: What about the other side of it; evidence to cast doubt on your views?

C: I know that even though I feel fat, objectively my weight is in the normal range. I know that even though I feel ugly, people have told me that I'm attractive. I think that when I am feeling fat and ugly, people may stay away from me because of the way I'm carrying myself, not because of my look, per se.

T: I think we just got somewhere. Why don't you write down the reasons to dispute your original view. You feel fat and ugly but receive feedback that you are attractive. You feel fat but your weight is in the normal range. When feeling fat and ugly you behave in a standoffish way so people shy away from you. Do I have it right?

C: Yes.

Step 4. Develop a Reasoned Conclusion Based on the Evidence

T: So, given your evidence to support and dispute, can you come up with a reasoned conclusion that counters your original problem thought?

C: I think so. It goes like this: "When I'm feeling fat and ugly it seems like people don't like me because of my looks, but really they are reacting to the way I am projecting myself because I feel unattractive." That's something I can work on.

Step 5. Determine a Course of Action Based on the Conclusion

T: How are you going to work on it?

C: Well, let's see. I think I would first be more alert to the thought of being fat and ugly, and second, when I felt that way I would watch the way I interact with people more carefully, to make sure I don't act standoffish. In that way I would stand less chance of feeling rejected by them.

Note: This could lead into a problem-solving exercise, helping the client to consider different ways to alter her "standoffish" behavior.

T: OK, let's write that down. With that conclusion in mind do you think that you would have left the situation not feeling the urge to binge and purge?

C: Yes. I wouldn't have felt so depressed and lonely afterwards.

T: Good. Why don't you try to identify another thought or two during the next week, and follow the method we have just used, writing it down on the back of one of your Daily Food Records. Then we can take a look at it in the next session.

It should be noted that clients vary in their ability to apply cognitive restructuring. Although the majority find this a useful approach, there are some clients who are not comfortable with the technique and find they cannot use it. The therapist should apply other procedures to deal with binge triggers for such clients.

Homework

The client should read Chapter 11 of the Client Workbook: *Challenging Problem Thoughts,* and complete a Challenging Problem Thoughts form as assigned in Exercise 11.1.

CHAPTER 17

Weight and Shape Concerns

One of the most important factors maintaining dietary restriction is the client's concern about weight and shape. Such concerns are fueled by low self-esteem which may stem from many different types of developmental problems. Often clients with Bulimia Nervosa have been teased about fatness, have been regarded as being overweight by their families, and so on. In the Western world today there is social pressure to achieve a thin body shape, which is unrealistic for most women. This gives rise to body dissatisfaction in many women who are of normal weight and who have a normative level of concern about body shape and weight. Hence, it is important to realize that it will not be possible to eliminate totally the client's concerns about weight and shape, although it should be possible to ameliorate such concerns.

There is a range of concerns about body shape in both the client with Bulimia Nervosa and the client with binge-eating disorder. Some clients demonstrate little more than normative discontent with their bodies, whereas others, especially those with a past history of Anorexia Nervosa, demonstrate gross distortion concerning weight and shape. Although clients believe their perceptions are "normal," they are usually much exaggerated.

The first step in treatment is to explore the client's thinking about his or her body shape in some detail. Doing so will usually be fairly simple because the client will have talked about some of these concerns already, and because he or she is likely to mention such concerns spontaneously in the course of treatment. It should be remembered that the client with binge-eating disorder also demonstrates distorted thinking about weight and shape. An example of addressing weight and shape concerns is given below. The therapist encourages the client to take a problem-solving approach to the weight and shape concerns associated with the minor weight gains that the client has made during therapy.

C: I purged because I was convinced that if I kept my dinner down, I would definitely gain weight, especially because I have been eating more regular meals and snacks and I have already gained 2 pounds since starting treatment. I feel like the weight gain is just going to continue endlessly.

T: I hear some distortions there. First, what did you eat for dinner, that you were so confident of an automatic, continuous weight gain?

C: Well, I was out for dinner with friends. I had half a salad, half of my serving of pasta, one glass of wine, two pieces of French bread, and I shared a dessert with a friend. I just thought that because I've already gained a few pounds, keeping down this dinner would contribute to my weight continuing to go up.

T: The dinner sounds pretty normal to me. But I'm hearing that you're afraid that you're going to keep gaining weight beyond the 2 pounds that you've put on, and you thought that this dinner would contribute to that process. I'm wondering if it's possible that you are exaggerating the effects on your weight of keeping down the dinner, and translating a 2-pound gain into a continuous trend upward in your weight?

C: Well it's possible, but I feel like it's the real truth—that I will continue to gain weight if I keep food like that down on a more regular basis.

T: Since you are open to the possibility that there is some distortion in your thoughts about the food and its potential to cause weight gain, how about we use the method to challenge problem thoughts to look at the evidence on both sides. You know the method; let's start with the first step, identifying the underlying problem thought, and take it from there.

C: OK. Step one, the underlying problem thought, is that "If I keep my dinner down, I'll continue to gain weight beyond the initial 2 pounds." Step two, the evidence to support, is that I did eat more fat than usual, the pasta had cream sauce on it and the dessert was a rich chocolate cake, and I felt really full after.

T: Is "feeling full" objective evidence that we can use here to support your thought?

C: Well I guess not, but I was really full and it made me feel as if I had eaten too much and would gain weight.

T: That may be yet another problem thought for us to address in a future session. But for right now, let's stick with this one. Is there any more objective evidence to support your belief that you'd gain weight upon keeping dinner down?

C: Yeah, there is. That I have gained 2 pounds already in the first several weeks of treatment, maybe because I have begun to eat more regularly. So that is evidence, along with the fact that it was a higher-calorie dinner than usual. So I guess we go to the other side now, step three, evidence to dispute or cast doubt on my thought. Um, the truth is, I hadn't eaten much that whole day. I had exercised quite a bit, so I probably really needed the calories that I took in at dinner. Also, I really did stick with half portions of everything, so that I took home

a doggie box to have for lunch the next day.
I ate much less than everyone else. And I'm
sure they didn't gain weight after eating their
food. I myself have eaten like this without gaining weight. And I know, based on that model,
that when I keep good meals like this down
I binge less frequently. So I'm really taking in
fewer calories. I also know that the 2-pound gain
might be just an arbitrary blip upward. I only
noticed it during the last weigh-in, and you
don't consider a weight gain to be significant
until you see it for 4 weeks. It might just be
fluid retention or something. So there is no
real reason to think that I would necessarily
have gained from that dinner or that an
uncontrollable gain is already underway.

T: Is there enough evidence to draw a reasoned
conclusion then?

C: Yeah, in step four, I guess I would say that first
off, even though I've "gained" 2 pounds it might
be an arbitrary gain since it only occurred during
one week's weigh-in. So certainly keeping down
one dinner, which was really moderately sized if
I think about, would do little as far as contributing to the gain. If anything, it would have just
prevented me from binge eating again, and
bingeing is what leads to weight gain more
quickly, because of all the calories. So I guess I'd
say that I'm probably not on an upward trend
with my weight and certainly the dinner would
not have contributed to an ongoing weight gain.

Other approaches to the problem of weight gain during therapy might
include an analysis of the pros and cons of gaining a few pounds versus
the costs of continuing symptoms of Bulimia Nervosa. Some clients,
particularly those with high dietary restraint and low weight, may need
encouragement to change the size of their clothes as they gain a few
pounds so that the tightness of clothing does not continually set off
worries about weight and shape. For the client with binge-eating disorder,

or the overweight client with bulimia, it is still reasonable to analyze the pros and cons of ceasing dietary restriction. However, such clients should develop a healthy lifestyle with a sensible exercise regimen and sensible alterations in food choices, rather than continue dietary restriction that leads to deprivation and hunger.

Overvaluation of a Slim Figure

Discrediting the cultural pressure to attain a thin body can sometimes be used to advantage with the client with Bulimia Nervosa. The therapist can point out that different cultures at different times have different ideals concerning weight and shape. In many cultures, including the Western world until recently, a more rounded, fuller body was regarded as ideal and as more feminine. It might be pointed out that biologically this shape is a more realistic expectation. Clients might be questioned as to whether they want to embrace inappropriate cultural expectations. In addition, the therapist might prompt clients to think more broadly about their good points outside of weight and shape, to begin to value such qualities more highly, and to spend more effort in developing them. Finally, clients might be asked to observe the figures of other women, whether at shopping centers or at the health club, while trying to maintain a realistic attitude. They will undoubtedly find that women come in many shapes and sizes, and that in this context their own concerns about weight and shape may be exaggerated.

Amplification of Ingrained Beliefs About Being Fat

As noted earlier in this chapter, many clients with Bulimia Nervosa have had a number of hurtful experiences concerning weight and shape, often over a considerable period of time. This process leads to a core belief that one is fat and unattractive. A negative mood stemming from a variety of causes can activate such beliefs. An example follows:

C: I felt like I might binge on Saturday. I went shopping and started trying on clothes and got a horrible case of feeling fat and ugly.

T: What was going on at the time that might have contributed to those feelings?

C: Nothing. It was just that I looked in the mirror after trying on some pants and I really did look horrible—fat and stocky.

T: Well did those feelings begin only after you tried on the pants or is it possible that you began your self-criticism some time before?

C: I usually get that way every time I shop. But, come to think of it, I tend to shop when I have nothing else planned, usually on a weekend, when I'm getting lonely and slipping into a bad mood. So maybe it actually started even before I left home, before I got to the store and tried on the pants.

T: What I'm hearing is that you had fallen into a low mood state because you had nothing planned on the weekend and were feeling lonely. You decided to go shopping to try to rouse yourself from this bad mood, but ended up feeling even worse, focusing all of the negative energy on criticisms of your body shape. Is it possible that you displaced some of the other, more complicated feelings—feeling down and lonely, not having plans—onto that familiar theme involving the concerns about your body weight and shape?

C: It is possible, but I really did look fat. But I guess maybe there was more going on. And if I knew that, and was able to step back a bit from my obsession with my body, I wouldn't have felt as tempted to do more binge eating and purging. I would have understood that my feelings were not really about the weight issue. And that would have maybe gotten me started on figuring out solutions for the real problems, like how to spend my time on weekends.

The use of one or more of these therapeutic strategies can do much to ameliorate the disturbed feelings concerning weight and shape that clients, including those with binge-eating disorder, exhibit. However, it is probably inevitable that the client will retain some degree of preoccupation about weight and shape. Nonetheless, by addressing this issue in the later stages of therapy, the client can gain an awareness of the unrealistic nature of such beliefs, and of the role that they may play in leading to the urge to binge.

Homework

The client should read Chapter 12 of the Client Workbook: *Weight and Shape Concerns*. The therapist should point out the exercises listing valued personal characteristics and physical attributes unrelated to weight and shape.

CHAPTER 18

Interpersonal Triggers and Transient Negative Mood

The antecedent event most frequently reported by clients with bulimia to trigger binge eating is a negative mood. Such moods usually arise from faulty interpersonal interactions, although clients may at first consider them to stem from disappointment with themselves, failure to achieve an impossibly high standard, general low self-esteem and so on.

Research suggests that transient negative moods have several effects. First, negative affect and negative cognitions appear to enhance the perception of loss of control over eating. Negative affect may be depression, anxiety, or anger. Negative cognitions may be about personal performance, such as "I'm a failure," or about the binge episode, such as "I'm a pig, I'm like an animal." Second, in a negative mood, clients are more likely to classify an eating episode as a binge, without taking into account the amount of food actually eaten. Third, it is also likely that in a negative mood clients overestimate the amount of food that they have eaten during the previous hours. As experiments with normal women who are on dietary restriction have shown, simply believing that they have eaten too much leads to overeating. Finally, many clients feel, rightly or wrongly, that binge eating offers an escape from and relief of their negative feelings. Indeed there is evidence that such moods do decrease in the short-term due to binge eating.

The client may note either the negative mood, a derogatory comment about performance, or an interpersonal interaction leading to a binge, on the Daily Food Record. There are several ways of approaching such episodes of transient negative mood. The faulty perceptions of bingeing or of the amount of food eaten can be challenged using evidence from the Daily Food Record. Negative cognitions can be clarified and challenged using the cognitive restructuring methods detailed in the previous chapter. When negative mood is related to interpersonal events, it is important for the therapist to help the client investigate the exact nature of the events leading up to the decision to binge eat. The best way to accomplish this is to work backwards from the immediate precipitant of the binge. If such events appear to be quite specific and often associated with binge eating, the problem-solving method can be used to find more adaptive alternatives for coping.

For example, it may be that the client becomes upset because her boyfriend does not call her, even though she is expecting to go out to dinner with him. This has two effects: first she becomes angry, and second she becomes hungry. Several coping methods may suggest themselves. The client might consider having a snack, or if the time is too late, going out for a meal by herself, preparing and eating a meal at home, or going out with a friend. Alternatively, better methods of coping with the anger or depression related to her boyfriend's behavior might be devised—for example, exercise, engaging in enjoyable behavior such as going out to a movie (after eating), a hot bath, etc.

It is also possible to take a broader approach to interpersonal problems. Given the example above, the therapist would help the client explore the nature of the relationship with her boyfriend, how they interact in general, and more specifically the details of the incident triggering the negative mood and binge eating. Having delineated the problem, the therapist can then suggest that the client try out new ways of interacting with her boyfriend over such incidents, and various alternative behaviors might be discussed. These new approaches to the relationship then become homework, and the results are reported at the next session, at which further exploratory work on the relationship may be necessary. However, it is important that this exploration should remain fairly tightly focused on interpersonal events that trigger binges, because there is not enough time during cognitive-behavioral therapy to explore fully and to resolve all troublesome aspects of such relationships. Straying too far afield may mean that essential elements of CBT are not covered adequately.

The client should learn that a negative mood is a warning that he or she may be at risk for a binge. Hence, the client should first attempt to clarify the reasons for the negative mood and then problem solve to find solutions, either for the negative mood or for the immediate risk for a binge. Problem solving for the negative mood may include an examination of distorted cognitions regarding the precipitant of the mood. In addition, if the client is at risk for a persistent negative mood, he or she should pay careful attention to eating three meals and two snacks at regular intervals to lower the risk of binge eating.

In summary, negative affect arising from faulty interpersonal interactions can be approached through cognitive restructuring, problem solving, or the more direct approach of engendering more successful interpersonal interactions. The therapist must choose the most helpful approach based on his or her assessment of the situation. The therapist will have a good deal of knowledge about the client's general interpersonal situation by this point in therapy, which will make it easier to choose an appropriate response.

The client should read Chapter 13: *Understanding More About Interpersonal and Emotional Triggers,* and the client's attention should be drawn to the chapter exercises, concerned with identifying mood and interpersonal triggers for binge eating.

SECTION 4

The Third Phase of Cognitive-Behavioral Therapy: Maintenance of Change

Relapse Prevention

The third phase of cognitive-behavioral treatment, prevention of relapse, spans the final three sessions of treatment. Other processes previously initiated should be continued, such as dealing with binge triggers and working toward preventing dietary restriction by tracking dietary intake. The session structure remains unaltered, beginning with a greeting and general inquiry as to how things are going, followed by a review of the Daily Food Records completed since the last session. Depending on the record review and the homework set in the previous session, the therapist should then set a specific agenda. This should form the main work for the session, and should be followed by a review of the main points covered, which should naturally lead to setting specific homework to be done before the next session. It is also useful to increase the length of time between sessions in this phase of therapy, seeing the client every 2 weeks, which allows the client a longer interval of time in which to experience and attempt to deal with residual problems.

In the first session in which relapse prevention is covered, the therapist should ask the client to consider what aspects of the program have been most useful in bringing binge eating and purging under control. This should be followed by asking the client to look ahead to the weeks and months following the end of treatment and to begin to identify the types of problems that might occur and lead to a lapse into binge eating, purging, or both. Finally, in preparation for the homework assignment, the client should be asked to think about ways of coping with such problems. The homework assignment is to develop a written plan for coping with situations that put the client at risk for binge eating, purging, or both, so as to maintain his or her improvements.

Within this discussion, the therapist should clarify the difference between a lapse and a relapse. A lapse is an episode of binge eating or bingeing and purging to which the client can apply problem-solving methods. A relapse, on the other hand, is a return of bulimic symptoms that persists for several weeks. By dealing promptly with lapses, a relapse can be prevented. Hence, it is important for the client not to catastrophize lapses by misperceiving them as a relapse, where all the gains made in therapy have been lost. The therapist should also point out to the client that there will be time in the last few weeks of treatment to test methods of dealing with some of the high-risk situations that could lead to ongoing binge eating. The client should watch for times when he or she has an urge to binge eat, especially if it does not lead to a binge. He or she should attempt to identify the precipitating circumstance and the methods used to avoid binge eating.

At the second session dealing with relapse prevention, the client's maintenance plan should be carefully reviewed and discussed in detail. If clients have had difficulty in finding solutions to some of the high-risk situations, the problem-solving method should be used within the session. Similarly, if the client has left out high-risk situations that the therapist knows about from past sessions, such situations might be discussed to ascertain whether they currently pose a high risk to the client. He or she should again be encouraged to test out some of the methods of coping with high-risk situations as they occur between sessions. In addition, as homework, the client should write a final maintenance plan based on the discussion within the session.

During this session the therapist should also broach the options the client will have after the completion of cognitive-behavioral therapy. Such options will differ for the successful and unsuccessful client and will therefore be discussed separately below.

The Successful Client

The successful client is likely to have ceased binge eating for the last few weeks of therapy, or to be binge eating only sporadically (usually binges of the subjective variety, i.e., small binges with a sense of loss of control). He or she should also have a good sense of the triggers for such binges, with a well-developed and adequate plan for coping with such triggers. Depending on their progress, successful clients might be offered further consultation if they experience renewed problems with their eating disorders with which they feel they cannot cope adequately. Clients who continue to binge eat sporadically can be told that there is an excellent chance that if they continue to apply the methods that they have learned during therapy, they will continue to see improvements over the next several months. Such clients might be offered further consultation when they feel it is needed, or they might be offered regular sessions on a diminished time course—for example, once each month—whichever they prefer. A plan for relapse prevention is important. Follow-up studies suggest that the months immediately following the completion of treatment appear to be a time of high risk for relapse (Agras, Rossiter, et al., 1994).

During the course of therapy the client and therapist might have discovered residual problems related to the eating disorder but outside the realm of cognitive-behavioral therapy. These problems might be interpersonal in nature. In such cases, the client and therapist might wish to address such problems in further sessions, although it should be clear to the client that treatment with cognitive-behavioral therapy specifically addressed to the eating disorder has ended.

Alternatively, recovery from the eating disorder might be accompanied by a recognition that a comorbid problem is now posing difficulties for the client. For example, because the client has more time to engage in behaviors outside of binge eating and purging, symptoms of a social phobia may become more prominent. In such cases, initiation of treatment for the comorbid condition or referral for treatment for that condition should be discussed with the client.

The Unsuccessful Client

It is hoped that some unsuccessful clients will have been identified at the midpoint of treatment, and an alternative or additional therapy modality has been put into effect with good results. For clients who continue to meet, or nearly meet, criteria for Bulimia Nervosa or binge-eating disorder, the options are much the same as those detailed in Chapter 12 of this Therapist Guide. The principal options are to add antidepressant medication, or, if it appears appropriate, to switch to interpersonal psychotherapy adapted for eating disorders. Any advice on this matter given to the client should be based on the clinical situation as it appears to the therapist and client.

Homework During Phase 3

The client should read Chapter 14 of the Client Workbook: *Maintaining Changes After Treatment,* completing the Therapy Progress Worksheet and the Summary of Progress exercise (Exercises 14.1 and 14.2) and developing a relapse prevention and maintenance plan (Exercise 14.3).

References

Agras, W. S. (1993). Short-term psychological treatments for binge eating. In C. G. Fairburn & G. T. Wilson (Eds.), *Binge eating: Nature, assessment, and treatment.* (pp. 270–286). New York: Guilford Press.

Agras, W. S., Rossiter, E. M., Arnow, B., Schneider, J. A., Telch, C. F., Raeburn, S. D., Bruce, B., Perl, M., & Koran, L. M. (1992). Pharmacologic and cognitive-behavioral treatment for bulimia nervosa: A controlled comparison. *American Journal of Psychiatry, 149,* 82–87.

Agras, W. S., Rossiter, E. M., Arnow, B., Telch, C. F., Raeburn, S. D., Bruce, B., & Koran, L. M. (1994). One-year follow-up of psychosocial and pharmacologic treatments for bulimia nervosa. *Journal of Clinical Psychiatry, 55,* 179–183.

Agras, W. S., Schneider, J. A., Arnow, B., Raeburn, S. D., & Telch, C. F. (1989). Cognitive-behavioral and response-prevention treatments for bulimia nervosa. *Journal of Consulting and Clinical Psychology, 57,* 215–221.

Agras, W. S., Telch, C. F., Arnow, B., Eldredge, K., & Marnell, M. (in press). One-year follow-up of cognitive-behavioral therapy for obese individuals with binge eating disorder. *Journal of Consulting and Clinical Psychology.*

Agras, W. S., Telch, C. F., Arnow, B., Eldredge, K., Wilfley, D. E., Raeburn, S. D., Henderson, J., & Marnell, M. (1994). Weight loss, cognitive-behavioral, and desipramine treatments in binge eating disorder. An additive design. *Behavior Therapy, 25,* 225–238.

American Psychiatric Association. (1994). *Diagnostic and statistical manual of mental disorders* (4th ed.). Washington, DC: Author.

Arnow, B., Kenardy, J., & Agras, W. S. (1992). Binge eating among the obese: A descriptive study. *Journal of Behavioral Medicine, 15,* 155–170.

Bruce, B., & Agras, W. S. (1992). Binge eating in females: A population-based investigation. *International Journal of Eating Disorders, 12,* 365–373.

Christensen, L. (1993). Effects of eating behavior on mood: A review of the literature. *International Journal of Eating Disorders, 14,* 171–183.

Cooper, Z., & Fairburn, C. G. (1987). The Eating Disorder Examination: A semi-structured interview for the assessment of the specific psychopathology of eating disorders. *International Journal of Eating Disorders, 6,* 1–8.

Eldredge, K. L., & Agras, W. S. (1996). Weight and shape overconcern and emotional eating in binge eating disorder. *International Journal of Eating Disorders, 19,* 73–82.

Fairburn, C. G. (1985). Cognitive-behavioral treatment for bulimia. In D. M. Garner & P. E. Garfinkel (Eds.), *Handbook of psychotherapy for anorexia nervosa and bulimia* (pp. 160–192). New York: Guilford Press.

Fairburn, C. G., Agras, W. S., & Wilson, G. T. (1992). The research on the treatment of bulimia nervosa: Practical and theoretical implications. In G. H. Anderson & S. H. Kennedy (Eds.), *The biology of feast and famine: Relevance to eating disorders.* (pp. 317–340). New York: Academic Press.

Fairburn, C. G., Cooper, Z., & Cooper, P. J. (1986). The clinical features and maintenance of bulimia nervosa. In K. D. Brownell & J. P. Foreyt (Eds.), *Handbook of eating disorders: Physiology, psychology, and treatment of obesity, anorexia, and bulimia.* (pp. 389–404). New York: Basic Books.

Fairburn, C. G., Jones, R., Peveler, R. C., Carr, S. J., Solomon, R. A., O'Connor, M. E., Burton, J., & Hope, R. A. (1991). Three psychological treatments for bulimia nervosa: A comparative trial. *Archives of General Psychiatry, 48,* 463–469.

Fairburn, C. G., Jones, R., Peveler, R. C., Hope, R. A., & O'Connor, M. (1993). Psychotherapy and bulimia nervosa: Longer-term effects of interpersonal psychotherapy, behavior therapy, and cognitive behavior therapy. *Archives of General Psychiatry, 50,* 419–428.

Fairburn, C. G., Kirk, J., O'Connor, M., & Cooper, P. J. (1986). A comparison of two psychological treatments for bulimia nervosa. *Behaviour Research & Therapy, 24,* 629–643.

Fairburn, C. G., Marcus, M. D., & Wilson, G. T. (1993). Cognitive-behavioral therapy for binge eating and bulimia nervosa: A comprehensive treatment manual. In C. G. Fairburn & G. T. Wilson (Eds.), *Binge eating: Nature, assessment, and treatment* (pp. 361–404). New York: Guilford Press.

Garner, D. M., Garfinkel, P. E., Schwartz, D., & Thompson, M. (1980). Cultural expectations of thinness in women. *Psychological Reports, 47,* 483–491.

Garner, D. M., Rockert, W., Davis, R., Garner, M. V., Olmsted, M. P., & Eagle, M. (1993). Comparison of cognitive-behavioral and supportive-expressive therapy for bulimia nervosa. *American Journal of Psychiatry, 150,* 37–46.

Kendler, K. S., MacLean, C., Neale, M., Kessler, R., Heath, A., Eaves, L. (1991). The genetic epidemiology of bulimia nervosa. *American Journal of Psychiatry, 148,* 1627–1637.

Klerman, G. L., Weissman, M. M., Rounsaville, B. J., & Chevron, E. S. (1984). *Interpersonal psychotherapy of depression.* New York: Basic Books.

Laessle, R. G., Beumont, P. J., Butow, P., Lennerts, W., O'Connor, M., Pirke, K. M., Touyz, S. W., & Waadt, S. (1991). A comparison of nutritional management with stress management in the treatment of bulimia nervosa. *British Journal of Psychiatry, 159,* 250–261.

Leitenberg, H., Rosen, J. C., Gross, J., Nudelman, S., & Vara, L. S. (1988). Exposure plus response-prevention treatment of bulimia nervosa. *Journal of Consulting and Clinical Psychology, 56,* 535–541.

Lieberman, H. R., Wurtman, J. J., & Chew, B. (1986). Changes in mood after carbohydrate consumption among obese individuals. *American Journal of Clinical Nutrition, 44,* 772–778.

Mitchell, J. E., Pyle, R. L., Eckert, E. D., Hatsukami, D., Pomeroy, C., & Zimmerman, R. (1990). A comparison study of antidepressants and structured intensive group psychotherapy in the treatment of bulimia nervosa. *Archives of General Psychiatry, 47,* 149–157.

Pike, K. M. (1995). Bulimic symptomatology in high school girls: Toward a model of cumulative risk. *Psychology of Women Quarterly, 19,* 373–396.

Pope, H. G., Hudson, J. I., Jonas, J. M., & Yurgelun-Todd, D. (1983). Bulimia treated with imipramine: A placebo-controlled, double-blind study. *American Journal of Psychiatry, 140,* 554–558.

Smith, D. E., Marcus, M. D., & Kaye, W. (1992). Cognitive-behavioral treatment of obese binge eaters. *International Journal of Eating Disorders, 12,* 257–262.

Striegel-Moore, R. H. (1993). Etiology of binge eating: A developmental perspective. In C. G. Fairburn & G. T. Wilson (Eds.), *Binge eating: Nature, assessment, and treatment.* (pp. 144–172). New York: Guilford Press.

Telch, C. F., Agras, W. S., Rossiter, E. M., Wilfley, D., & Kenardy, J. (1990). Group cognitive-behavioral treatment for the nonpurging bulimic: An initial evaluation. *Journal of Consulting and Clinical Psychology, 58,* 629–635.

Wilfley, D. E., Agras, W. S., Telch, C. F., Rossiter, E. M., Schneider, J. A., Cole A. G., Sifford, L. A., & Raeburn, S. D. (1993). Group cognitive-behavioral therapy and group interpersonal psychotherapy for the nonpurging bulimic individual: A controlled comparison. *Journal of Consulting and Clinical Psychology, 61,* 296–305.

Wilson, G. T., Eldredge, K. L., Smith, D., & Niles, B. (1991). Cognitive-behavioral treatment with and without response prevention for bulimia. *Behaviour Research & Therapy, 29,* 575–583.

Yanovski, S. Z. (1993). Binge eating disorder: Current knowledge and future directions. *Obesity Research, 1,* 306–324.